Most Wanted and Offstage Theatre in association with
W14 Productions, Alastair Michael and Soho
(co-commissioners) present

# THE POLITICAL HISTORY OF SMACK AND CRACK

## ED EDWARDS

*The Political History of Smack and Crack* was first performed
at Paines Plough's Roundabout at Summerhall
as part of the Edinburgh Festival Fringe on 3 August 2018

The production is kindly supported by Arts Council England,
the Fidelio Charitable Trust, the Unity Charitable Trust and The Mustard Tree

THE POLITICAL HISTORY OF
**SMACK AND CRACK**
ED EDWARDS

## Company

MANDY                          Eve Steele
NEIL                           Neil Bell


WRITER                         Ed Edwards
DIRECTOR                       Cressida Brown
LIGHTING DESIGNER              Richard Williamson
SOUND DESIGNER                 Jon McLeod
  AND COMPOSER
MOVEMENT DIRECTOR              Kate Sagovsky
COSTUME CONSULTANT             Esteniah Williams
PRODUCER                       Annabel Williamson, W14 Productions
PRODUCER                       Alastair Michael
STAGE MANAGER                  Rachel Graham


Paines Plough's Roundabout at Summerhall,
Edinburgh Festival Fringe
3–26 August 2018

Soho Theatre, London
4 –22 September 2018

The Mustard Tree, Manchester
1–17 November 2018

# Cast

### Eve Steele | MANDY

Eve trained at The Arden School of Theatre, Manchester.

Theatre credits include: *Life by the Throat* (Underbelly and national tour); *Trial* (Reveal Season, Octagon, Bolton); *The Manchester Project* (HOME); *Multi Story* (Octagon, Bolton); *Lub You* (24:7 Theatre Festival, Octagon Bolton, Young Vic); *A Little Local Difficulty* (Oldham Coliseum); *Newspaper Boy* (53:TWO); *Habeas Corpus* (Octagon Bolton) and *Criminals In Love* (Contact).

TV and film credits include: *Scott and Bailey*; *Sleeping Lions*; *Granddad's House*; *The Driver*; *The Visit*; *Doctors*; *Accused*; *AWOL*; *Tidy*; *Spooks: Code 9*; *The Royal*; *Blue Murder*; *Playing the Field*; *Peak Practice*; *Fat Friends*; *Casualty*; *This Filthy Earth* and *Coronation Street*.

Radio credits include: *Brief Lives*; *My Brother Michael* and *The Limits of Dominion*.

As a writer Eve has written a number of stage plays, short films and radio plays. In her first stage play, *Lub You*, Eve played the lead role of a two-year-old boy. The show was directed by Ed Edwards and was nominated for several awards. Eve won a Manchester Theatre Award for her performance in this piece and since then she and Ed have gone on to collaborate regularly and founded their own theatre company, Most Wanted.

### Neil Bell | NEIL

Neil trained at Oldham School of Performing Arts and Darlington College.

Theatre credits include: *Tony Teardrop* (Cut to the Chase Productions); *The Bubbler* (King's Arms, Salford); *Bluebird* (Salford Arts Theatre); *15 Minutes With You, Paper Boys* and *The Weir* (Studio Salford); *Miracle* (Greenroom, Manchester); *Crying In The Chapel* (Contact) and *Oh What A Lovely War* (Coliseum Theatre, Oldham).

Television credits include: *Broken*; *No Offence*; *Houdini and Doyle*; *Cuffs*; *This is England 90*; *Moving On: Scratch*; *The Last Trace*; *Knifeman*; *Peaky Blinders*; *Downton Abbey*; *Moving On: True Love*; *World Without End*; *Hustle*; *The Other Child*; *The Visit*; *I'm With Stupid*; *Ideal*; *Twisted Tales: Flat 4*; *The Street*; *City Lights*; *Blue Murder*; *Dead Clever*; *Donovan*; *11th Hour*; *Sex Traffic*; *Coronation Street*; *Lenny Blue*; *Simone Valentine*; *Sunshine*; *Skies of Glass*; *Doctors*; *Casualty*; *Olaudah Equiano*; *Drama Class*; *League of Gentlemen*; *Strumpet*; *Nice Guy*; *Eddie*; *Stretford Wives*; *When I Was Twelve*; *Married, Single, Others*; *Victoria Wood Christmas Special*; *The Chase*; *Blade Camp*; *Emmerdale*; *The Ghost Squad*; *Shameless*; *Murphy's Law*; *Deepcut: A Perfect Place For Murder*; *Buried*; *Second Coming* and *State Of Play*.

Film credits include: *Peterloo*; *Quadraturin*; *Swallows and Amazons*; *Pan*; *Victor Frankenstein*; *Powder*; *Weekender*; *Outlaws*; *Dead Mans Shoes*; *Touched*; *As We Ran*; *Getting Off*; *Death Of Klinghoffer*; *Me, You and The Dead*; *Opiate Awareness* and *24 Hour Party People*.

For radio: *Find Me* and *Sir Ralph Stanza's Letters From Salford* (Radio 4).

# Creative Team

### Ed Edwards | Writer

Ed has published five novels, a children's book and worked for various continuing TV dramas. He has had several original plays broadcast on Radio 4 as well as short films on Channel 4 and BBC2. He is co-artistic director of Most Wanted Theatre, which he runs along with Eve Steele. Ed recently directed another Most Wanted show, *Life by the Throat,* which received a string of five-star reviews at the Edinburgh Fringe.

### Cressida Brown | Director

Cressida Brown is the Artistic Director of Offstage Theatre who since 2006 have been dedicated to celebrating unheard voices. Extensive outreach always goes hand in hand with their incendiary productions and they have commissioned, developed and directed premieres with over 28 emerging and established playwrights.

Offstage is probably best known for: *Amphibians* inspired from interviews with former Olympic swimmers and staged in the hidden pool under the Bridewell Theatre stage; *Home* based on interviews with former residents of the Beaumont Estate towers and staged promenade around one of their towers pending demolition; *Walking the Tightrope: The Tension between Art and Politics* a series of short plays presenting polar opposite opinions on freedom of expression by writers including Caryl Churchill, Timberlake Wertenbaker, and Mark Ravenhill; *Phaedre* adapted to reflect the testimonies of the local community Craigmillar and staged promenade throughout the Craigmillar Castle ruins in Edinburgh.

Theatre credits include: *Septimus Bean and His Amazing Machine* (Unicorn); *caught* (Arcola) and *Almost not Quite* (Tricycle). Internationally she has directed *The Tempest* (RSC, Ohio), *Konchia* (British Council, Georgia), *Macbeth* (Barde-en-Seine, Paris) and *Theatre Uncut* (Theatre Row, NY). This year she will direct *Twelfth Night* in China for the Guangzhou Dramatic Arts Centre and RSC.

www.offstage.org.uk

### Richard Williamson | Lighting Designer

Richard trained at the London Academy of Music and Dramatic Art.

Theatre credits include: *Great Expectations* (national tour); *Lock and Key* and *I Have A Bad Feeling About This* (Vault Festival); *Fiddler On The Roof* (Istanbul); *Beowulf, Jason and the Argonauts* and *Septimus Bean and His Amazing Machine* (Unicorn); *Strangers In Between* (Kings Head); *Insignificance, Thebes Land, Drones, Baby, Drones, Shrapnel: 34 Fragments of a Massacre, Mare Rider* and *Happy Ending* (Arcola); *Boris: World King* (Trafalgar Studios); *The Body* (Barbican Centre); *Rotterdam* (Trafalgar Studios, Theatre503 and New York; Olivier Award for Outstanding Achievement in an Affiliate Theatre); *Easter Rising* (Jermyn St Theatre); *Brenda* (High Tide and The Yard); *Dusty* (Charing Cross Theatre); *Thrill Me:*

*The Leopold and Loeb Story* (UK and international tour); *La Trashiata, The Dispute, The Man Who Almost Killed Himself* and *Sleight & Hand* (Hibrow at Edinburgh Festival) and *Ha Ha Holmes* (Jamie Wilson Productions).

Opera credits include: *Ballo: A Masked Ball* and *Tosca* (Kings Head) and *La Boheme* and *The Mikado* (Charing Cross Theatre).

Richard is Head of Production for C venues at the Edinburgh Festival, Technical Manager for the Greenwich and Docklands Festivals and develops industry iOS applications such as PlayFadePause and Shift-Label.

## Jon McLeod | Sound Designer and Composer

Theatre credits include: *Ross & Rachael, Spine, Tribute Acts, A Conversation, The Fanny Hill Project, Penguinpig, Tell Me Anything* (UK tour); *Food, Just To Get Married, I'm Gonna Pray For You So Hard* (Finborough); *Macbeth, Followers* (Southwark Playhouse); *Arthur's World, The Rest Of Your Life* (Bush), *Fair Field, Party Skills for the End of The World, 66 Minutes in Damascus* (Shoreditch Town Hall); *Brutal Cessation, Dark Room* and *Screens* (Theatre503); *If We Had Some More Cocaine I Could Show You How I Love You* (Old Red Lion); *Strangers In Between* (Trafalgar Studios), *Eyes Closed Ears Covered* (The Bunker); *Free Fall* (The Pleasance); *Stink Foot* (The Yard) and *Heartbreak Hotel* (The Jetty).

## Kate Sagovsky | Movement Director

Kate has worked extensively as a movement specialist for companies such as Paines Plough, and at venues including the National Theatre, the Barbican, and the Southbank Centre. In 2011 she was Resident Movement Practitioner at the Royal Shakespeare Company. As Artistic Director of Moving Dust, Kate has directed a number of new works including: *This Much [or an Act of Violence Towards the Institution of Marriage]* (Soho, Ovalhouse and Zoo Venues); *The Box* (Bush); and *Sometimes There's Light [Sometimes There's Dark]* (The Place,Dance City and Ovalhouse).

## Esteniah Williams | Costume Consultant

Esteniah graduated from Mountview Academy of Theatre Arts in 2018 where she studied Theatre Production Arts BA. This is her first professional production.

## Rachel Graham | Stage Manager

Rachel trained at Rose Bruford College of Theatre and Performance.

Theatre credits include: *Night at the Oscars* (Aria Entertainment); *Aladdin* (Qdos Productions); *31 Hours* (The Bunker); *Some Lovers* (The Other Palace): *Treating Odette* (Upstairs at the Gatehouse); *Lonely Planet* (Tabard and Trafalgar Studios); *Jam* (Finborough); *Posh* – All Female Production (Pleasance London); *Pyjama Game* (Urdang Academy at Pleasance London); *Cinderella* (First Family Entertainment); *Magnificence* (Fat Git Theatre); *Down to Margate* (Joseph Hodges Entertainments); *Sweeney Todd* (Royal Academy of Music) and *Sister Act* (Curtain Call Productions).

### Annabel Williamson | Producer

Annabel Williamson is the founder of W14 Productions, focusing on new plays with a strong social conscience. Most recently *31 Hours* (The Bunker), *Jam* (Finborough), *The Brink* (a co-production with the Orange Tree), *The Late Henry Moss* and *Upper Cut* (Southwark Playhouse).

### Alastair Michael | Producer

Alastair is an emerging creative producer in Manchester. He graduated from the Liverpool Everyman's Young Producers Scheme and founded Ransack Theatre, with which he produces Northern premieres of contemporary plays, most recently winning Best Fringe Production at the Manchester Theatre Awards 2017.

Soho Theatre is London's most vibrant venue for new theatre, comedy and cabaret. We occupy a unique and vital place in the British cultural landscape. Our mission is to produce new work, discover and nurture new writers and artists, and target and develop new audiences. We work with artists in a variety of ways, from full producing of new plays, to co-producing new work, working with associate artists and presenting the best new emerging theatre companies that we can find.

We have numerous artists on attachment and under commission, including Soho Six and a thriving Young Company of writers and comedy groups. We read and see hundreds of scripts and shows a year.

'The place was buzzing, and there were queues all over the building as audiences waited to go into one or other of the venue's spaces... exuberant and clearly anticipating a good time.' Guardian.

We attract over 240,000 audience members a year at Soho Theatre, at festivals and through our national and international touring. We produced, co-produced or staged over 40 new plays in the last 12 months.

As an entrepreneurial charity and social enterprise, we have created an innovative and sustainable business model. We maximise value from Arts Council England and philanthropic funding, contributing more to government in tax and NI than we receive in public funding.

Registered Charity No: 267234

Soho Theatre, 21 Dean Street
London W1D 3NE
Admin 020 7287 5060
Box Office 020 7478 0100

Supported using public funding by
**ARTS COUNCIL**
**ENGLAND**
LOTTERY FUNDED

# OPPORTUNITIES FOR WRITERS AT SOHO THEATRE

**We are looking for unique and unheard voices – from all backgrounds, attitudes and places.**

**We want to make things you've never seen before.**

Alongside workshops, readings and notes sessions, there are several ways writers can connect with Soho Theatre. You can

- **enter** our prestigious biennial competition the **Verity Bargate Award** just as **Vicky Jones** did in 2013 with her Award-winning first play *The One*.

- **participate** in our nine month long **Writers' Labs programme**, where we will take you through a three-draft process.

 **submit your script** to submissions@sohotheatre.com where your play will go directly to our Artistic team

- **invite us** to see your show via coverage@sohotheatre.com

We consider every submission for production or any of the further development opportunities.

**sohotheatre.com**

Keep up to date:

sohotheatre.com/mailing-list
@sohotheatre all social media

# SUPPORTERS

Jonathan Glanz and Manuela Raimondo
Alban Gordon
Andrew Gregory
Fawn James
John James
Shappi Khorsandi
Jeremy King OBE
David and Linda Lakhdhir
Mike Lee
Jonathan Levy
David Macmillan
Nicola Martin
Adam Morley
Phil and Jane Radcliff
Sue Robertson
Dan Ross
Chantel Sinclair-Gray
Garry Watts
Andrea Wong
Matt Woodford
Henry Wyndham
Christopher Yu

## Soho Theatre Comedy Friends
Oladipo Agboluaje
Fran Allen
Adele Ashton
James Atkinson
Polly Balsom
Uri Baruchin
Antonio Batista
Katie Battock
Cody Benoy
Georgia Bird
Kieran Birt
Peter Bottomley
Matthew Boyle
Rajan Brotia
Christie Brown
Joni Browne
Jesse Buckle
Indigo Carnie
Chris Carter
Paul Chard
Roisin Conaty
Vanessa Cook
Grant Court
Sharon Eva Degen
Niki di Palma
Jeff Dormer
Amanda Farley
Peter Fenwick
Sue Fletcher
Stephen Fowler
Cyrus Gilbert-Rolfe
Terry Good
Robert Grant
Eva Greenspan
Steven Greenwood
Gary Haigh
Irene Hakansson
John Hamilton
Colin Hann
Anthony Hawser
Gillian Holmes
John Ireland
Alice Jefferis
Nadia Jennings
Nicola Johnson

Jo Jolley
Anthony Kehoe
Julie Knight
Andreas Kubat
Simon Lee
Ian Livingston
Amanda Mason
Neil Mastrarrigo
Roy Mclean
Chris McQuiggin
Laura Meecham
Lauren Meehan
Ryan Miller
Robert Mitchell
Richard Moore
Mr and Mrs Roger Myddelton
James Nicoll
Alan Pardoe
Simon Parsonage
Andrew Perkins
Keith Petts
Edward Pivcevic
Nick Pontt
Jessica Prebble
Ashwin Rattan
Gareth Rees
Paul Rogers
Graeme Rossiter
Natalia Siabkin
Ed Smith
Harriet Smithson
Hari Sriskantha
Sarah Stanford
Jennifer Stott
Lesley Symons
Andrew Thorne
Rocco Vogel
Gabriel Vogt
Anja Weise
Mike Welsh
Matt Whitehurst
Alexandra Williams
Kevin Williams
Allan Willis
Kirsten Wilson
Maria Wray
Liz Young

Soho Theatre has the support of the
Channel 4 Playwrights' Scheme
sponsored by Channel 4 Television.

We are also supported by Westminster
City Council West End Ward Budget
and the London Borough of Waltham
Forest.

*We would also like to thank those
supporters who wish to remain
anonymous*

**Mustard Tree**
Combatting Poverty – Preventing Homelessness

Mustard Tree has an established track record over the past twenty-five years, supporting people across Greater Manchester in poverty and facing homelessness. In 2014 our work was recognised with our organisation receiving The Queen's Award for Voluntary Service.

We exist because chronic poverty, extreme inequality, and severe disadvantage exist.

At Mustard Tree we believe everyone should be able to feed themselves and their family, live in a secure home, be healthy, find meaningful work and have the chance to discover their talents.

We create opportunities for people to help themselves through providing practical support, friendship, connections into work and improvements to health and wellbeing, alongside new experiences to encourage aspiration.

To find out more please visit our website:
www.mustardtree.org.uk

# Thanks

Special thanks to Eve Steele who dramaturged the play, helped develop the character of Mandy and halfway through the whole process wrote the first scene.

*The Political History of Smack and Crack* has been generously supported by Arts Council England, The Unity Trust, The Fidelio Charitable Foundation, The Mustard Tree and Synergy Theatre Project.

Thank you also to Bolton University, Dick Bonham of LittleMighty, The Gate Theatre, HOME, The Lowry, Manchester Royal Exchange, Paines Plough, Stone Nest, Theatre503, The Unicorn, Adam Tizroutine, Mark Gilman, Imogen Ashby, Esther Baker, Suzanne Bell, Charlotte Bennett, Adam Brace, Carolyn Brown, Matt Eames, Paul Fox, Jenny Hughes, Anoushka Graham, Jez Green, Steve Harper, Graham Hudson, Councillor Beth Knowles, Lynsey O'Sullivan, Lisa Spirling, Roy Williams and Joanne Wilson.

# THE POLITICAL HISTORY OF SMACK AND CRACK

Ed Edwards

**Bold = male actor (mostly Neil)**

Neutral = female actor (mostly Mandy)

*Italics is live dialogue whether **bold**... or neutral.*

Lines can be reassigned as seen fit, taken as stage directions, etc.

*(There are also occasional stage directions in brackets for clarity.)*

This edition features the full-length version of the play.
A slightly shortened version was first performed at the Edinburgh Festival Fringe.

*This text went to press before the end of rehearsals and so may differ slightly from the play as performed.*

**1.**

1875, Connecticut, USA.

**A woman is carried into a hospital, screaming.**

Agony. An iron fist squeezing the breath from her body.

**Chest caved in, ribcage smashed.**

Hollow, hopeless, hysterical.

**From the hefty wooden wheels of the stagecoach and all the weight of three fat New Yorkers – *BANG* – and down and over and disaster!**

Sound of her own bones breaking, crunch and crack and shock.

**And here she is and the doctor, shaken, looks at the bloody breathing mess before him.**

The blood-curdling cries, scraping jagged against his eardrums, and he says,

*Pass me the vial that Henderson just brought in.*

And the nurse opens a leather pouch and there's a tiny glass bottle and the doctor gets a syringe.

**And plunges it into the clear pure liquid and draws up…**

*Mmm.*

**And taps and squirts a tiny drop.**

And the nurse says, *Is it safe?*

**And the doctor says, *She's dying*.**

And the vein is found and the needle meets, punctures, slips inside.

**A little blood, drawn back, tumbles like a thin scarlet ribbon into the gleaming crystal solution and then…**

Down, the thumb presses gently, the liquid slides easily,

**The magic goes to work.**

A rush, a flooding, relief and heaven and the pain lets go its evil gnashers and a sigh: *Thank God, maybe, I'll be, will I? Who cares? Thank God, the pain, releases the grip of, the agony, thank God, the torture, thank…*

**And she's gone, but at least it's with some peace.**

Not screaming terrified into the hereafter, but slipping, sighing, surrendered.

**The fight gone.**

The giving up glorious.

**In the goodbye to life and plunging to eternal sleep is an element of ecstasy.**

And the nurse says, *Doctor, what was that, in the vial?*

**And the doctor says, *It's new, an opiate, very powerful painkiller. We'll see if it catches on.***

And the nurse picks up the tiny glass vial and looks closely at the label. *Heroin.*


*Eh-up!* (NEIL *cheekily pockets the vial.*)

**2.**

Manchester. Present day.

**He's not what he was, Neil.**

He's not.

**He bends over a bit now, like this.**

Bit of an old crock. (*To* NEIL.) *He bends over more than that!*

**Mandy's even worse.**

She's seen better days, yeah. But she's not as bad as Neil.
Fuck's sake!

**She's younger than Neil is.**

*What's that gotta do with it?*

*I'm just saying.*

She's definitely not what she was. She's not.

**She was good in her day though.**

*Now you're talking.*

**Gorgeous actually.**

She didn't know it back then though.

**She knew it alright.**

Yeah she did. She had a top arse back then.

**It's still not bad Mandy's arse. Even now.**

*Thank you very much.*

**Even though, some days, Mandy's on a walking stick.**

*It's a crutch!* And it's not because she can't walk that, it's this condition she's got.

**Yeah, it depends on the conditions whether she's got it or not.**

Walking stick! Sounds worse than it is that does. Comes in handy though her stick, when she needs it.

**Take the other week.**

Take the other week for instance. And this proves, by the way, on a good day, she's still got what it takes.

**Out shopping she is.**

*Shoplifters of the world unite.* As Mandy always says.

**It's Morrissey who says that.**

Yes but Mandy doesn't just say it. She's out there doing it.

**Take the other week for instance.**

There she is coming out of Boots on Market Street, minding her own business, when this brawny security guard accosts her – cheeky bastard, staring at her chest like that.

**Then she realises.**

Her boobs are lumpy.

**There's this shower gel she can't resist.**

L'Occitane – *Neroli and Orchid*. It doesn't fit up your sleeve… (*So down her bra it goes.*)

***Step back inside the shop with me will you please, madam.***

*Sorry my kids are waiting for me up there, they're gonna be worried.*

***Don't make me put my hands on you love*, he says with a certain relish.**

*I'm not going anywhere, am I, not on this.*

**She wafts her stick at him.**

Her stick's like this charm redefining her in the public mind, making her seem harmless, vulnerable even.

**Her five-inch heels are the problem.**

Not exactly running shoes. The stick's her only hope.

**It's weighted. She's had the end off, put a bit-of-something inside, glued it back on. It's heavy.**

It's not that heavy.

**It is when it cracks you unexpectedly in the face.**

Like that. *Crack!* (*In the Guard's face.*)

*Fffockinell! – BANG!* **The loudest crack is his head hitting the deck. An old lady nearby gasps.**

*Oooh!* Mandy's off up Market Street stumbling on her heels like a dickhead. She just knows, behind her, the security guard's gonna be up in like one – two –

*Three!* **He's up! Humiliated by the attention the old dear's trying to give him, Terry – he's called Terry the guard – gives chase.**

Outside Urban Outfitters by now, Mandy's all knees and elbows and arse sticking out, and – she can't help it – she does a little wee in her knickers. And she knows it's stupid but she just can't let go of her shoes. They're so cute and expressive of who Mandy is, and she's got so attached to them since she robbed them from Russell and Bromley last week –

She catches the eye of this bunch of lads...

**It's one of Mandy's skills that, catching the eye of a whole bunch of lads.**

She's like, bang – *Hiya lads* – quick as a flash – *Anyone got a light?* Fags out. *Want one anyone?*

**Terry can't see – well, he can see Mandy alright – but the rest of the world's lost in a mist. *BOOM*. Rugby tackle. *Ooof!* The feel of Mandy's body under his great weight**

**reminds Terry of the throb of a fish on the end of his line when he was out with his dad as a boy. Funny, that.**

I mean it's not nice is it? Great lump like that knocking the breath out of you when you're talking to a nice bunch of lads on Market Street. Big mistake really.

**The first thing Terry knows about the 'nice bunch of lads' is a sharp pain in his right hand. Worse than the one on his face.**

I mean they're nice lads. Mandy doesn't know he's got a knife, the dead pretty one. And I mean he doesn't even need to use it.

**He doesn't need to use it because Terry's hand's trapped under the big ugly one's foot.**

Mandy kicks her shoes off now, because, well she's got time. She grabs the beautiful velvet straps and legs it barefoot into the Northern Quarter. *See ya.*


*That's where it all changed, the Northern Quarter that day.*

*Is it?*

*You know it is!*

### 3.

**He was a rum cunt in his day, Neil.**

It's not nice that, is it.

**It's how he was known round his way. Neil thinks it's funny.**

It might be funny, but it's not nice.

**He was an' all. Proper rum.**

He was. Mandy remembers it only too well.

**She was there.**

Sometimes she was. He wishes it could've been more. But she wasn't in to him.

**His daddy was a rum bugger too.**

A rum bugger who give rise to a rum cunt.

**Example.**

Chemist.

**Nantwich.**

He has a car then, Neil.

**Yeah, borrowed it.** (*Wink.*) **It's quieter out that way, and so's the security.**

Manchester was on top by then.

**So we drive across to Nantwich.**

Bumper falls off on the way.

**Neil tosses it over the hedge, drives on.**

It's quiet. Nice.

**Nice people out this way. Decent quality of life.**

People stare at you when you get out of the car, though.

*Fuck 'em.* **Chemist's a cinch.**

Neil cuts his arm on the glass on the way in.

**Fair dos though, eh. Bandage. Savlon. Wipes –** *No safety pins? What kind of fucking chemist is this?*

Mandy's like, Alarm's going off, suddenly he's St John's fucking Ambulance! *Come on!* She does her famous little wee.

**It's a deep cut, he's still got the scar. Anyhow. We get the dangerous drug box, lug it over the wall.**

Mandy gets her tights stuck on the glass at the top.

**That's when we see 'em. The cops.**

There's a ripping sound. Mandy clunking painfully down on her heels.

**Blue flashing lights on the buildings up the street. We've got twenty seconds, tops.**

(*Re:* NEIL*'s car*.) It's wrong to call it a car at all really.

*Won't start. Shit! Get out. Push it!*

*What!? I've got five-inch heels on here!*

*Fuckin hell. Do it myself then.*

Neil pushes the thing a few yards down the street. Mandy sort of hops along next to him.

*Get in!*

We crouch there while four police cars turn up, do a lot of talking and radioing, someone comes to fix the window and they all just drive off.

**Never occurs to them to just look in the parked car.** (*High-fives?*)

We drive back to Manchester.

**Starts first time.** *It was good that little car.*

Then it's, Drug box!

**Lid off.**

*Beautiful.*

**Like breaking into a sweet shop when we were kids.**

Which we did by the way.

**Ate sweets till we were sick, and then ate more till we were sick again.**

I still can't face a Sherbet Dip Dab to this day. Was that the first time they ever committed a crime together?

**Let's say it was. It's romantic.**

Not for Mandy. They were never an item Neil and Mandy.

**They did have sex.**

No they didn't.

**Yeah they did.**

Well it didn't mean anything to Mandy if they did.

**Whereas Neil can't stop thinking about her for weeks. Back then he only has to envisage her legs and his belly aches.**

Not Mandy's type.

**Which never stops her shagging a lot of other guys who aren't her type.**

(*Changing the subject.*) Drug box. *Go on then!* (*Meaning: let's take something.*)

**Milk of paradise.**

Bottles.

**Pills...** *Where the fuck's the morphine?*

*No fucking morphine!*

*No pethidine!*

*No methadone!*

**Fuck. All!**

Bottles, pills, bottles, pills… (*Throwing them everywhere.*)

*Shit! Maybe the labels are wrong?*

*You idiot! I told it you it was the wrong box!*

*Fuck it, let's try summing, come on.*

Neil gets out his works, shoves it in a bottle, *bang*. Straight into his arm. Then?

(*Fit of agony from* NEIL…)

*What's it like? Is it any good?*

(*Same again from* NEIL…)

*Neil! What's it fucking like? Is it any good?*

(*Gurgling.*) **It's fucking fantastic! Best hit I've ever had!… Auurrgh!**

That's good enough for Mandy, she's like, works, bottle, *bang*. Then… *Arrgh!*

**Gurgling. Spasms. Dribbling. It's not nice.**

Fucking agony! Every fibre on fire. It goes on for ages. She can't see! She thinks, *This is it!* When eventually it stops she says, *Why the fuck did you tell me it was good!*

**Neil just shrugs, and says, *I didn't want to die on my own.***

*Twat.*

**Rum.**

Twat.

**4.**

Mandy grabs the beautiful velvet straps of the gorgeous five-inch heels she stole from Russell and Bromley and legs it barefoot into the Northern Quarter.

**Terry – the security guard – doesn't follow because his fingers are still trapped under the big ugly one's foot.**

The guys cheer as Mandy goes.

(*Cheer.*)

She does her best to give them a little wiggle in gratitude. They're nice guys.

**And there he is.**

At first she's not definitely sure it's him.

**He's standing there staring at her.**

Gormless.

**How long is it since they've seen each other?**

It's not so much the length of time, as the rate of deterioration.

**As a heroin addict Neil holds it together for thirteen years, more or less, in a hard-bitten-junkie kind of way. Crack puts him on his arse in two years flat.**

Mandy puts her shoes back on. Makes sure he clocks her best side.

**He still doesn't have a clue who she is.**

She stands up. Five inches taller.

**Something inside Neil stirs. *Mandy?***

*It is you then. Look at the fucking state of you, you tramp!*

*That's not very nice.*

*Whorr! And you stink! What's the matter with ya?*

**It's only a week since Neil was stripped stark bollock naked on Market Street thinking he was Jesus Christ. But he hasn't had crack since because his cheque isn't due, so he's only on methadone and prescription-medication-he-hasn't-got-a-prescription-for,**

So when he says:

*I'm alright, what you on about!*

He genuinely believes he is.

*You look good*, he says.

*Do you think so? I got these in Russell and Bromley last week.*

*It's not the shoes, girl.*

She lets him look at her. Sees a shadow of the old familiar look on his face. But then she gets this feeling she can't identify.

**Mandy's eyes are shining. Her face is all clean. To Neil, post-Jesus Christ on Market Street, she looks like the archangel Gabriel, female version.**

*I'm clean,* she says.

*Yo! Me too, girl!*

*I mean I'm totally clean. I've had nowt.*

*Yeah yeah, me too. Me too.*

She just laughs. He can hardly stand up the twat. *Come for a coffee.*

*Can't, girl. Got places to be and all that. Things to do.*

*Like what?*

*Well you know, bit of this, bit of that. You know the score.*

Pity. The feeling's pity. This is the guy people used to look up to. *I'm not asking you. You're coming for a coffee, yeah.*

*I'd love to, girl, but you know how it is.*

*Yeah and it's like this: You might not've smoked a rock but you're off your tree on meth, you tosser. You've got nowhere to go, fuck-all to do, no friends, not even anyone you can rip off, so you're coming for a coffee and no excuses, yeah?*

**And she turns and she struts away.**

Her best strut. No stick.

**Neil follows, like she knows he has to.**

**5.**

**It's not even a proper coffee bar.**

When she walks in, they hug Mandy like she's some sort of superstar.

*Yo, Mandy, where you been since yesterday, we've missed ya, gal.*

*You can let go now, Mikey.*

**There's all these rogues there – well and some nice people. Neil knows some of them, the rogues.**

*Alright, Neil, fucking state of ya, man!*

*You been sleeping in a skip or what?*

*I thought you was dead, you twat. Someone dig you up for the day?*

*I'm alright, what you on about?*

Neil doesn't realise he's been tricked into his first Narcotics Anonymous meeting.

**He also doesn't realise he's become:**

Mandy's New Project.

**See, none of Mandy's new friends know about Mandy's shoplifting exploits.**

Not that they'd judge her if they did.

**They'd judge her alright.**

They would actually. They'd say things like,

*If nothing changes nothing changes…*

*To get clean you gotta change your playthings, your playgrounds and your playmates, yeah?*

*People, places and things...*

It annoys Mandy when they say shit like that.

**It makes her reluctant to tell the truth about how she spends the long, empty, terrifying days before a meeting.**

Shoplifting.

**Seeing a couple of her old punters. But now:**

Project!

*What the fuck is this place, Mandy?*

*Just sit down for a bit and listen, yeah?*

**It's half an hour before Neil even gets that it's all about drugs.**

She wants to laugh at him. She sees the moment when it hits home.

*You're not even allowed weed or alcohol!?!*

He tries a bit of attitude, but she can see he's listening.

*Dickheads.*

There's this one guy with Aids and Hep C, blind in one eye, lived out of skips for years, teaches kids with learning difficulties now. When he tells his story Neil sort of grunts like that:

*Umph.*

Mandy's on the edge of her seat willing him to get it. It's a thrill.

**Tattooed Martin's on him as soon as it's over.**

*Yo, dickhead, you're staying at mine tonight, yeah.*

**Neil tries his, *Got places to go,* and all that, but:**

*Nah you haven't.*

**He knows Neil from Strangeways prison, Martin does. He takes Neil home to his new house, *very nice*, runs him a bath.**

*Get in, you stink.*

**He introduces Neil to his wife, gives him clean clothes and a bed in his spare room.**

*Touch my kids and you're dead, right!*

***Like I'm gonna do that!***

Next morning Mandy kidnaps Neil, heading off his escape attempts with casual flirting –

**She's good at that –**

Until it's evening, Neil's had nothing all day and there's another meeting.

**It goes on like that for days.**

And she hasn't been shoplifting once.

**He's feeling rough by now. He gets through it by concentrating on Mandy's legs.**

He starts to listen properly in meetings. She can tell from the not-quite-so-gormless look on his face.

**He finds a bit of hope from somewhere.**

And Mandy shares about her shoplifting in a meeting.

**But not the punters.**

*It's not punters, it's just one guy and he's dead nice. He gives me lifts. He's lovely actually.*

**He's in love with you.**

*I like him, he's kind.*

***Whatever.* Neil gets some of his old spark back, stands up a bit straighter again.**

They go for a picnic at the waterpark.

**Mandy buys iced fingers.**

She gets the woman in Gregg's to butter them.

*I fucking love iced fingers!*

*I know you do.*

**It's beautiful out there. And this is not a word Neil uses lightly. If ever.**

They talk about old times.

**Nantwich and all that.** *I never said that!*

*Yeah you did.* (*Impression.*) *I didn't wanna die on my own.*

*It's not nice that, is it.*

*It's not, Neil, no. And it's not funny.*

*I know.*

*So why you laughing?*

*Do you remember coming swimming here when we were kids with all the lads?*

*No?*

*You took your jeans off and jumped in off that wooden thing over there.*

*No way! I'd never do that. Must've been someone else.*

*It was definitely you. I remember it well. Very well indeed.*

*Twat.*

**For a few days, it is, it's beautiful.**

Which is why it's such a shock – such a disappointment – such a death within a death – when two days later Mandy finds Neil dead on the floor of Martin's spare room.

**6.**

**You can't buy heroin on the streets of Manchester in 1981.**

Liverpool, Manchester, Brixton, Bristol. You can't get hold of it.

**Unless you're in the music business.**

Or you've been travelling in Asia and you've got the balls to bring it through customs.

**Basically there's ex-students and misfits dabbling with China White and that's it.**

In the whole of Britain there's two thousand heroin addicts.

**Three thousand, tops.**

Soho. Rock bands. The families of the rich.

**The heroin that kills Neil is a different story.**

One that starts on the 8th of July, 1981, at a precise moment in time.

**2 a.m. At a precise location.**

The pawnbroker's shop on the corner of Raby Street and Princess Road in Moss Side.

**By coincidence, Neil is there the moment it all starts. Right at the epicentre.**

By coincidence, Mandy passes by with her mum ten minutes before.

**Neil is twelve years old, but he looks ten.**

Mandy's six but she thinks she's sixteen.

**1.50 a.m.**

Mandy's walking to A and E with her mum. Her mum's broken her arm and doesn't want to admit how she did it cos it's not her fault she needs a bit of something to take the edge off now and then...

### Neil's staring in the pawn-shop window at a Sony Walkman.

As Mandy and her mum walk past, Mandy's mum thinks, vaguely, *What the fuck's a kid doing out on his own at this time?* Mandy stares at him. She remembers it years later, when she realises what happened that night, there was a boy there, out on his own.

### Big shop window. Yellow light from the lamp post. Boy.

It's vivid. When they get to A and E, Mandy's mum's devo-ed because the doctor gives her a fiver out of his own pocket for a taxi home: It obviously shows.

### 2 a.m. exactly. Neil's still there outside the pawn shop. He could see it coming if he looks up. But he's too busy bumming a cig off Irish Tony.

Nowt's changed there then.

*Come on, Tony, I'm gasping!*

*Fuck orf!*

### That's no way to talk to a twelve-year-old, but Irish Tony's had two Nembutal and half a bottle of cheap whisky so what does he care.

And anyway, what the fuck *is* a twelve-year-old boy doing out on his own at that time?

### As the white van pulls up outside the pawn shop, Neil grabs the packet of cigs and laughs in Irish Tony's face.

It's more about winding Irish Tony up than about the cigs.

### A white man emerges from the van and walks towards the shop.

Irish Tony grabs the little get by the wrist.

**Neil yelps,** *You old bastard!* **But –** *CRASH!*

This is the moment. The epicentre.

**The white man from the van puts a brick through the pawn-shop window.**

Neil and Irish Tony stop fighting and stare.

*CRASH!* **Neil pockets the cigs.**

It's 2 a.m. on a Wednesday night, but suddenly there's young people everywhere.

**Young people who love the sound of breaking glass.**

This is the epicentre of unemployment.

**This is the epicentre of Peter Tosh:** *Wanted Dead or Alive.*

The epicentre of police harassment.

**The epicentre of people who've had enough of cops kicking them around.**

The epicentre of the 'sus' laws and Operation Swamp.

**This is the epicentre of people who love the sound of breaking glass.**

The epicentre of Margaret Thatcher's England.

**This is the sharp end.**

This is – *CRASH!*

**This –** *SMASH!*

The white man from the van puts a brick through the pawn-shop window and –

*BOOM!*

Neil feels a violent leap of ecstasy in his chest.

**The history of Manchester jumps off its axis.**

The history of England jumps off its axis.

**July. 1981.**

Every major city in England burns.

**Birmingham, Liverpool, Manchester, Bristol, Leeds, London north, London south...**

A beautiful, burning ecstasy of rage.

**Some say.**

A snarling upsurge of *fuck off* to the cops who've been waiting round in their vans, spoiling for it for weeks. Some say.

**Some say they're spoiling for it that night, the bastards:**

By coincidence, Neil sees them, earlier, outside that club,

**The Nile on Princess Road,**

*It'll never go off in Manchester*, the cops taunt.

*It'll never kick off here in Manchester! Never kick off here!*

But when it *does* come – and it does come –

**They can't take it.**

They're shocked by the scale of it.

**They lose Liverpool completely.**

They have to fight their way back *into* Liverpool.

**In Moss Side, Manchester, a thousand people surround the police station.**

The hated Greenheys Lane.

**The cops have to fight their way *out* of Greenheys.**

And in the middle of it all, a twelve-year-old boy with a spike of ecstasy in his heart.

**There's a thousand – ten thousand – spikes of ecstasy out on the streets that night.**

Enough to sink the whole rotten, bastard stop-and-search kick-you-when-you're-down lot of them.

**There's a moment.**

Mandy and her mum, arm in a sling, threading their way home through the scary backstreets, avoiding the screams and the sirens – but Mandy's had enough.

**Neil, in a sea of youths. He can't believe it, they're hurling rocks, bins – anything – they're throwing fire!**

Mandy, a few streets away refuses to go another step. *No more walking, NO!*

**Neil, rock in hand, steps into the empty space between youths and cops – the yawning no-man's-land – a great cheer erupts behind him.**

Mandy's mum thinks, *Should have got that fucking taxi!* But a fiver's a fiver.

**A couple of the cops laugh at him, this tiny little kid marching at them with his grin and his freckles.**

*It's a bottle that. Or forty cigs. Or food for half a week.*

**This tiny little kid in the middle of the madness.**

*Come on, Mandy, please, love!* But Mandy's angry face says it all. She could say no back then.

**But this tiny little kid hurls his rock at them with all the force of his ancestors.**

Her mum heaves Mandy up with her one good arm and staggers on groaning with the effort. Mandy instantly asleep.

**It's just a stone really. But it crashes onto this copper's shield and he flinches and drops it, and the youths take courage and charge in a screaming mass at the line.**

*(Cheer.)*

Mandy's mum hears this cheer from a few streets away where it's dark and there's no one. Or so she thinks.

**They run. The whole bastard line of coppers run for their fucking lives.**

That's when she sees three youths, scarves up, hoods down, coming over out of the dark.

**One of the coppers trips. Neil's the first to catch up to him. It's the one who flinched and dropped his shield.**

The one with the scarf up's got a knife, Mandy's mum sees it glinting slyly in the dark.

**The cop's on the ground. Neil stands there staring at him.**

Mandy's mum stares at the kids. *Shit. My fucking fiver!*

**Later on Neil tells people he gives the copper a kick. But he doesn't. He just stands there feeling like a giant.**

The kid pulls his scarf down and says, *You want me to carry her for you, miss?*

**The cop gets up and scarpers with the rest of them.**

Mandy's mum says *Thanks, love*. The kid gives Mandy a piggyback. And in the distance the burning.

**The burning.**

The burning.

**Before this you can't buy heroin on the streets of Manchester.**

Not a single, beautiful, brown crystal of it.

***That's* when it all changed.**

**7.**

It's good though, init, smack.

**It's alright.**

The first time she tries it Mandy thinks, *This is me now*. She knows straight away she never wants to stop.

**Neil just pukes his ring and doesn't bother with it for months.**

She claps her hands together like that and says, *That is what I need. I am taking that every fucking day and I don't care.* She thinks: *It's like the missing piece of me.*

**Eventually Neil sort of just goes along with it because it's everywhere by then and everyone's doing it.**

Dickhead. For me it's like, that noise in my head. It stops. Just like that. (*To* NEIL.) *So what, you don't even fucking like it?*

*It's alright.*

*You think it's 'alright' and you spend the next ten years running round after it?*

**Yeah and you think it's great till your boyfriend stops bringing it home for you. How long's that last?**

*About two weeks.*

**Then what?**

*Then I go out and score on my own.*

**You go round to your ex's. It's always been about a man for you.**

*I don't know any dealers at the start.*

**And when he gets sick of you, what then?**

*Shoplifting.*

**And are you any good at it?**

*Top actually.*

**But?**

*But I keep getting caught.*

**So what then?**

*A car stops and I get in. What's your point?*

**It's because of you Neil starts on it.**

*Fuck off!*

**He's heartbroken when you leave him.**

*I'm never <u>with</u> him!*

**You spend three months together.**

*We're mates.*

**You sleep in his bed.**

*Sometimes I do.*

**You have sex with him. He remembers it like day.**

She doesn't remember it at all.

**The night it happens, it takes Neil by surprise. He's been mad about her since they were kids. He wants to savour it.**

Faintly.

**He doesn't even go all the way – he's saving it for the next night. He doesn't know it's a one-off.**

Mandy has sex with a lot of guys she doesn't want to have sex with back then.

**What, why?**

*It's complicated.*

**So, you don't wanna have sex with Neil but you do it anyway?**

*Maybe I want it that first night.*

**But not the second?**

*No.*

**But I thought you have sex with guys you don't wanna have sex with!**

*I feel safe with Neil.*

(*Frustrated and baffled,* NEIL *gives up.*)

**That second night Neil can tell she's not up for it, so he stops. When she falls asleep in his arms he doesn't move in case she wakes up and rolls away. After ten minutes his arm goes dead but he stays there all night. *What a dickhead.***

*Don't say that.*

**He wants to cut his dead arm off and leave it there wrapped around her forever.**

It was just never gonna happen.

**He knows that now.**

She stops going round.

**And Neil gets nicked, gets six months.**

Mandy's a mess by then. Too much whizz and acid and Es and craziness. She's paranoid to fuck and heroin fixes that.

**For two weeks. Then she runs out of money and boyfriends and exes.**

And she gets in that car.

**It's like someone's switched the lights off. *What about Nantwich?***

*Nantwich is a high point. There are a few.*

**When Neil gets out he goes round to his mate's and his mate says,**

*Want some?*

**And Neil thinks, *Why not.* There's two weeks when it's alright, and later there's Nantwich, and then there's nothing but shit.**

She remembers all this, Mandy does, when she finds Neil in the Northern Quarter and takes him to a meeting.

**She's thinking about it the morning she comes to Martin's house a couple of hours before she finds Neil with a needle in his arm and no pulse.**

She's thinking how safe she felt. How she feels safe again now.

**Neil's thinking about Mandy that morning, too.**

On his way to work, Tattooed Martin has a friendly word for him on the subject: *Get a male sponsor, stay away from Mandy.*

*I will, I will, it's just, you know, we go back, we get on.*

*You've been saying that for weeks. She may as well be a bottle of whisky, a pill, or a dig…*

**Translation:**

Dig. To inject oneself, for example with heroin. As in, 'To have a dig.' Or: (*Back to it.*) *She may as well be a bottle of whisky, a pill, or a dig!*

*We're mates, me and Mandy, we always have been.*

*You can't be mates with a woman, Neil, it's bollocks.*

**It's a retro statement that. Neil doesn't believe it, he doesn't want to hear it and he's worried it might be true.**

*She's bad news.*

*She's not like a proper woman.*

Martin just gives him a Strangeways stare.

*You can really talk to her. She's one of the lads. She's done the things I've done.*

*So you're a prostitute now?*

*What?*

*I've seen the way you look at her. Everyone has. You're a disgrace.*

**Neil thinks:** *She's coming round in a bit, I'll talk to her then.*

*When are ya seeing her?*

*Tomorrow night, at the meeting, I'll talk to her then.*

*Sex and drugs, man. When ya first get clean it's the same thing. People relapse over this shit, it's serious.*

*I'll tell her.*

*The things you've done and you're crying over a woman.*

*I'll tell her.* **Fuck's sake!**

Because of his old reputation people are harsh with Neil. They don't know him like Mandy does. He's always had a thing for her, and who can blame him. It's his fatal flaw.


**And for the record, last time Neil cried he was nine years old.**

**8.**

*Bottle of whisky, pill or a dig. Bottle of whisky, pill or a dig.*
*Bottle of whisky...*

*Neil.*

**Mandy!**

Hug.

**Big hug.**

*You can let go now, Neil.*

**Oh, right, sorry yeah, right. Right.**

*What's the matter with you? You're acting weird.*

**Nothing. Do you wanna brew? Brew, yeah, make a brew.**
**Make a brew. Make a brew – there. Brew.**

*Neil. What the fuck?*

**I made you a brew. Drink.**

*There's bits.*

**What?**

*Floating. Lumps of summing.*

**Shit, milk's off, throw it away. Sit down, come on. Or shall we**
**go out. Let's go out.**

*Why are you being a dick?*

**What you on about?**

*Has someone said something?*

**What? No.**

*'Stay away from Mandy, she's bad news.'*

**He's genuinely gobsmacked.**

*'She may as well be a bottle of whisky, a pill, or a dig.'*

**He's a dickhead. I don't listen to him.**

*It's alright. We can leave it for a bit. You can go to a few more meetings.*

**I go every night as it is. Fuck off. No one tells me what to do.**

*They're not telling you. It's a suggestion. They say it to everyone.*

**He's bad news, talking to me like he owns the place. The fact that he does has got nothing to do with it.**

*It's probably not a good idea.*

**What's not?**

*Spending all our time together.*

**You don't want to?**

*Course I do.*

**Well then. Fuck 'em. It's nice. Like old times. Better.**

*Yeah.*

**You're not so paranoid.**

*Yeah and you're not gonna go out and get in a fight.*

**And we're not gonna get nicked any minute.**

She tries not to pull a face.

**You've been out 'shopping' again?**

*It was a one-off.*

**Maybe you are bad news.**

*Maybe I am.*

**Who does he think he is? It's none of anybody's business how we spend our time.**

*He's just jealous.*

**Yeah. Wait. Jealous?**

Oops.

**Oh.**

*Let's go to the waterpark.*

**Neil doesn't feel nice. Or like going to the waterpark.**

*Are you alright?*

**When was it?**

*A while back.*

**How long had you been clean?**

*A few weeks. But it was me. I made a beeline for him. He's just my type, int he.*

**What? Bastard?**

*Unavailable.*

**He wasn't though was he. Even though he is!**

*I feel terrible about it now.*

**It's wasn't your fault! He's been clean years, you were new around.**

*I can handle myself. It was a one-off. Well, a three-off.*

**Something is fucking wrong with Neil's stomach.**

*<u>Are</u> you alright?*

**There's something he's got to say, but it's stuck in his stomach.**

*Neil, what is it?*

**Kiss me.**

*What? No.*

**Come on, Mandy. This is bullshit. I love you. No one's ever loved you like I do.**

*That's the problem.*

*Kiss me.*

*No!*

*What's wrong? I'm better looking than most of your exes – fucking all of them!*

*You'll regret it.*

*I won't. I can handle myself, you know I can. My fucking hands are shaking.*

*Come on then.*

**Neil realises he's never kissed anyone sober before. Literally ever.**

Mandy gets another feeling she can't identify.

**He thinks,** *Did she kiss Martin?*

*Stop. Kissing you's weird. Feel my tits instead.*

*Okay.* **Neil's assaulted by sensations, including: that this is just skin and flesh.** *Is that alright?*

*Slightly less weird.*

*Let's get into bed, come on.*

*I don't think we should.*

*Course we should, why not?*

Mandy doesn't know what to say, or how, or anything any more.

*I'll be fine, don't worry. We won't tell Martin.*

(*She starts to undo her jeans.*)

*That's it, go on. Come here.*

*Do you know what, let's leave it.*

*What? No way, we've started now, take these off.*

*Maybe in a few weeks, eh.*

*We'll do it once then and leave it for a bit, yeah?*

*No, stop now. It's a bad idea.*

**Mandy, we need this, I love you. Fuck, I'll pay you if that's what you want!**

*(Screams at him.) Fucking stop! Did you not hear me! I said no! Fuck's sake!*

**Oh shit! Oh fuck! What am I doing? Fuck!**

*It's alright.*

**I'm sorry. I thought you wanted it. I don't know what's the matter with me.**

*It's alright. I said no. You stopped.*

**I've always had a thing for you.**

*I know.*

**Come on, let's go out.**

*No. Let's leave it for a bit.*

**Yeah, yeah, you're right. Let's leave it.**

*A few days.*

**Yeah. A few weeks if you want.**

*Will you be alright?*

**Course.**

*Phone someone.*

**I will. I will.** The door closes – and it's not nice.

Mandy walks to the bus stop crying. Cries at the bus stop. Gets on the bus.

**By the time he's found the money in Martin's wife's knicker drawer, nothing's gonna stop Neil scoring.**

Three stops and Mandy realises what's definitely gonna happen next. She jumps off the bus and runs back towards Martin's house.

**After he finds the money he thinks,** *It's not enough.* **Finds her jewellery.** *That'll do it.*

When she gets back to Martin's house the front door's unlocked.

**On his way to score, on his way back, if he sees anyone, he'll just lie. Maybe not to Mandy.**

When she sees the mess she works out where he's gone to score and sets off after him.

**Once he's scored Neil thinks,** *I'll go back to Martin's, tidy up, have a dig, pretend I'm napping. Go to a meeting later.*

When Mandy gets to the dealer's it's the wrong place. *Fuck!*

**Neil goes back to Martin's, doesn't bother to tidy up, gets out his works.**

*Where the fuck will he go? Back there! Shit!*

**Even as he's cooking up Neil wishes he could stop it. But he's so disgusted with himself, on so many levels, it's impossible.**

She runs all the way, smashing her heart on her ribcage. *Fucking heels!*

**On her way to Martin's, every move Neil makes, every thought he has, Mandy sees it, and knows it, and she's right.**

She phones Martin, but it's too late.

**Neil's already dead.**

**9.**

### The day after it all burns in Manchester.

Bristol, Birmingham, Liverpool, and all that.

### 9th of July, 1981.

Thatcher's Home Secretary, William Whitelaw himself, comes to Manchester.

### He's photographed amid the scorched carcasses of cars in the exact spot where Neil stood over the fallen cop feeling like a giant.

His picture's on the news that night. Grim face.

### Blackened moonscape of rocks and rubble.

Important-looking cops.

### The next day they come back hard.

It's like an occupation.

### One of the lads on Neil's street sees his cousin in a police uniform. His cousin's in the army.

They stop the post for a week, no one gets their giro.

### Anyone young and black leaving the estate gets picked up – even though it was nearly fifty-fifty white and black on the night.

They come for the kids first, it's easier to get names off them.

### They scream to a halt next to Neil on the Saturday, in five vans, but he's thin enough to squeeze through some railings and get off at the back of the City ground.

Irish Tony explains it to him later.

### He's seen it all before.

*(Unintelligible.) If you stand up to them they gotta come down on ya, or why wouldn't ya do it again.*

**Give us a cig, Tony.**

*Fuck orf.*

**After a week there's a lot less of them,**

But the gloves come off.

**They come in quick, break a door, grab someone, get out quicker.**

Lurking like blue lizards at the edges of the area.

**Cowering in vans with cages on the windows.**

Hold your breath when they pass, if they stop leg it, if they don't stop leg it anyway.

**They pick up a twelve-year-old black lad, hold him till midnight, then empty his pockets and drop him in whitest Salford on his own.**

4 a.m. Thursday night they stop a local reggae sound system on their way back from a gig.

**Twelve coppers haul them out, smash their speakers, break a wrist, beat the whole crew up – charge them all with police assault.**

It's a tipping point.

**Parents, preachers, youth-club leaders, even Neil's teacher form a defence committee for the sound-system crew.**

Youths who've been arrested come for help and get it and soon half the estate are involved.

**The committee organise a demo at the police station against the random arrests. Neil tags along for a laugh.**

Minister Jackson organises TV cameras to be there.

**Cops stay inside.**

Three hundred people gather outside the Magistrate's Court in town when the sound system lads are up for police assault.

**They all get out on bail and there's talk of the charges being dropped.**

They come out to a massive cheer – and there's a ragtag march back to Moss Side.

**The atmosphere changes. When the cops come into the estate now, kids like Neil are off on bikes, or running round sounding the alert.**

Mandy's at her auntie Joyce's with her mum when it comes to a head.

*Police! Nobody move, stay where you are!*

Three vans, four cars outside Joyce's.

**Eleven cops inside, looking for Joyce's thirteen-year-old son Darren.**

They look scared – of two women and a six-year-old girl!?

**They're rude.**

They break Joyce's plate, with the picture of Pope John-Paul on it.

**They rummage in drawers and open cupboards.**

*You won't find our Darren in a cupboard,* Joyce taunts.

**Then it happens.**

The cops feel it as much as hear it.

*BANG* **– half a brick on the roof of a van outside.**

One old copper with a fat belly left outside gets the fright of his life.

**The rest still inside, like that:** (*Scared stiff.*)

Radios crackle – *urgent!*

**Running up, Neil sees the angry crowd ahead – his mates who've got bikes are there already.**

So many of us, so quickly!

*BANG* – **car roof!**

*CRASH* – van window!

**And here they come.**

Lizard uniforms scrambling, batons drawn. Pale frightened faces. And not without reason.

**That's when Neil sees him.**

The cop from that night, who dropped his shield and fell.

**The one he stood over feeling like a giant.**

Then *SMACK*! The cop's lip explodes into red. Blast of colour.

**It's a shock, vivid in Neil's mind. He doesn't like it suddenly.**

Well over a hundred of us by now!

**And the noise!**

Screaming, shouting, crashing, banging.

**Police van doors slamming. Engines. Violent revving.**

A woman so nearly killed as the first van screams away – and another, and two of the cars.

**But then the cheering as they go! And Neil suddenly happy again.**

And the best thing?

**The thing every one of them'll remember forever.**

The dancing when they realise it.

**Like when City came back up only this is us doing it ourselves.**

The two patrol cars they leave behind.

**One of them's over on its roof by the time they turn the corner at the top of the street.**

They must have seen it, the bastards.

**Someone hot-wires the other one and they take turns driving it up and down the street for hours. They get on the radio and taunt the control.**

And then they burn that one too.

**A seven-foot antique hunting horn is fetched out from somewhere and this mad old white guy sounds it like the fog horn on the Titanic.** (*Hoots*.)

Then it's speakers.

**Music.**

Barbecue.

**Whole families are there.**

Black. White. Some Asian lads.

**Even Mr P from the corner shop with a few free packets of sausages.**

His was one of the places that didn't burn.

**People stood outside to make sure. He's alright is Mr P.**

It's like: burning police cars. Street party.

**The anti-Jubilee.**

If they come back tonight surely the whole world's gonna burn.

**But they don't. And somehow everyone knows they won't.**

**10.**

**It's now exactly two minutes, twenty-five seconds since Neil's heart stopped beating in Martin's spare room.**

Mandy turns the corner at the top of Martin's street. She trips and falls, cutting her knee, losing five seconds...

**Martin's house is forty yards from the end on the left.**

Mandy knows he's dead, she can feel it.

**But at the same time...**

*'I've died three times, me.'*

**He sits up and listens the first time he hears that in a meeting, Neil does.**

*'Died three times.'*

**It makes him feel he's in the right place, surrounded by the right people for once, because well, this isn't the first time Neil's been found dead either.**

This isn't the even the first time Neil's been found dead by Mandy. How long does the human brain survive after the heart stops beating?

**Up to ten minutes, but after four – forget it.**

So from when she trips at the top of the street, Mandy's got exactly ninety seconds to get oxygen into Neil's brain...

**But there's a problem. If Mandy does save Neil...**

They immediately become an unrepresentative sample of addicts in recovery.

**Because most of us who get clean don't stay clean.**

So one of us'll still probably die?

**Statistically the odds are against.**

But that's not gonna stop Mandy trying now is it.

**No.**

Which gives us exactly ninety seconds to get through the politics…

**11.**

So get this.

**The ruined moonscape of Manchester makes a visible impression on Home Secretary Whitelaw.**

You can picture him in the Home Office reading reports of the growing resistance in Manchester with care, face set, that grim look.

**Pencil cross in the margin. Underlining one of the words.**

'Organised.'

**Writing something of his own in the margin.**

*Bin…*

*Lids.*

At this time bin lids are used by women in Northern Ireland to warn of the approach of British soldiers.

**Reports like that would go with Whitelaw to the next full cabinet meeting.**

It's the biggest story in the country.

**And a few seats away from him at the famous polished table?**

Margaret Thatcher herself.

**Picture her sitting there, eyes shining, talking in low tones to a representative of the Foreign Office about two things before the meeting gets under way.**

The revolution in Nicaragua.

**And the fight against communism in Afghanistan.**

In both places, Thatcher supports the right-wing opposition gangs who are struggling to survive – mainly cos they're such a bunch of bastards.

**But there's these two other reports,**

Right there on the table with the ones from Manchester,

**Saying that the Nicaraguan opposition gangs are shipping huge quantities of cocaine to the US – soon to become crack,**

And that heroin is about start flowing into Britain from Afghanistan, refined and transported by the forces Thatcher supports there.

**The question *isn't*, by the way,**

How do we prevent this potential catastrophe?

**The money's essential to keep both forces going. The issue is,**

How to stop the information getting out.

**When the meeting gets underway things would be tense.**

There's a hunger strike by IRA prisoners in Northern Ireland.

**A hundred thousand people march behind the coffin of the first man dead.**

There's revolutions all over Africa.

**Apartheid is in crisis.**

Latin America's on fire.

**El Salvador, Guatemala,**

Argentina, Chile,

**Granada, Colombia, Peru.**

They're literally losing the world.

**And right here, right now,**

People with nothing to lose are burning cars and buildings and fighting the police in their very own England.

**During the discussion of the 'Inner City Disturbances', Whitelaw would surely consider mentioning developments in Manchester.**

Because it always starts with the small stuff,

**These Nicaraguas and Afghanistans,**

These Cubas and Angolas.

**With the banging of cooking pots,**

Argentina.

**The crashing of bin lids,**

Ireland.

**A visit to a mosque,**

Palestine.

**The unveiling of women in public places,**

Afghanistan. The teaching of a language,

**Kurdistan.**

The Black Panthers start by conducting traffic at a dangerous junction.

**But whether or not Whitelaw mentions the defence committee, or anything else in Manchester...**

Or Birmingham, or Brixton, or Leeds...

**The gravity of the situation is clear to everyone in the room.**

Within weeks the head of the army in Northern Ireland becomes head of the army in Britain,

**And the chief of the Northern Irish police becomes the head of the Met in London.**

And together they reorganise the whole system of policing to ensure as little as possible is left to chance.


*That was well more than ninety seconds.*

*Was it?*

**12.**

**It's not the fact that Martin's front door is still open.**

Or that Mandy knows from experience what to do when she finds Neil dead on the floor in Martin's spare room.

**It's not the pumping of his heart. Oxygen to his brain and all that.**

Fucking twat's turned blue!

**It's not the way she keeps her head and dials nine-nine-nine on her mobile in between the puffing and pumping.**

It's none of that stuff that gets Mandy,

**When she's sat by his bed all night in the hospital,**

And it's dark but for the lights of the city in the distance and he wakes up and sees her there,

**And he says, *Mandy! I didn't think I'd see you again.***

And,

***When I stuck it in my arm I thought, 'That's too much,' but I carried on anyway.***

And she says, *I thought you'd died.*

**And he's says, *I'm a twat.***

And she says, *You're a fucking twat.*

**And he's says, *Come here.***

And she puts her head on his chest,

**And it hurts but he likes it.**

It's only <u>after</u> all that.

**When Mandy goes back to her lonely flat,**

And gets a feeling she can identify as soon as it hits her,

**Slaps her,**

Punches her in the gut.

**When she realises.**

Clear as fucking day.

**She's fallen in love for the first time in her life.**

*Fuck!*

**And she cries,**

Huge, convulsive sobs.

**She doesn't cry because she's fallen in love. Not even because she's never fallen in love before.**

That's what starts it, but it's not what really gets her.

**They all think he'll get out of the hospital, go straight back out there, never see him again.**

But Mandy knows Neil better than they do. He'll think,

*I'll show 'em.*

He'll do it right this time.

*No Mandy. Meeting every night.*

Voluntary work.

**He'll get down on his knees and pray to a God he knows doesn't exist.**

He'll see Mandy at meetings sometimes, but they'll keep it friendly.

**They'll give each other just enough eye contact to know, underneath, nothing's changed.**

But then, six months later.

**Nine months.**

A year even.

**However long it takes him to feel strong enough.**

He'll come to her and he'll say,

*I'm ready.*

She runs the scenario through her mind, honing it. This is the bit she sees the most clearly, the bit that really gets her:

**She won't be able to resist him.**

She'll think, *I shouldn't.*

**But she'll do it anyway.**

And the kissing.

**And the fucking.**

It'll be good for Neil, she'll make sure of that.

**It'll be good for her too.**

Different. Scary. But nice. Probably.

**She'll feel his love for her, big time.**

She'll like it and she'll try and hold on to it.

**For a time,**

It will. It'll be nice.

**It'll be the nicest thing that's ever happened to them. Best thing ever.**

But she knows what she's like.

**The damage has been done.**

It's that thing about men that Neil picks up on but takes the wrong way when he says,

*It's always been about a man for you.*

He's right and he's wrong.

**When that car stops and the guy offers her money for sex, she doesn't think:**

*How come I can do this?*

**She just cuts herself off and gets on with it.**

She's already cut off.

*As a percentage, how many women heroin addicts were abused as kids, d'ya reckon?*

*Definitely the ones who do what Mandy did.*

**Does. She doesn't connect the cutting off now to what happened when she was little.**

But she feels it when she gets home from the hospital that night.

**It's why she cries so hard.**

She sees it clear as day:

**He'll get stronger and come to her.**

She won't be able to resist, or even want to.

**They'll do beautiful things for days and weeks, months even.**

Then, she'll destroy him.

**13.**

**Right enough, next day Mandy goes back to the hospital.**

She should phone someone and tell them she finds the days too long and empty, but…

**She doesn't. And guess who's there?**

(*It's Tattooed Martin.*) *No good all this, is it, Mandy. No good at all.*

**Mandy's like,**

*It's not, Martin, is it.*

**She can see Neil through a window to the side, being tended to by a doctor, looking frail and pathetic.**

*He was in me wife's knicker drawer, that's a big no-no for a woman, he's an idiot and a danger to other people.*

*Did you tell your wife about you and me, yet, Martin?*

*That's a fair point, Mandy, and I don't blame you for making it but no.*

*Where's he gonna go, do you know?*

*Probly come knocking at your door now, drag you down with him.*

Something about Martin being there and the doctor and Neil looking wizened and stupid in the bald light of day says,

*Walk away and stay away.*

As she goes she gets a giddy feeling and her belly lurches.

**She doesn't stop to think what the feeling is.**

She just thinks: *Neroli and Orchid* and heads into town.

**In Boots she realises she's not alone.**

The voice is back, whispering in her ear.

***Go on, take it.***

*I've already got six of these.*

***Sixteen quid for a shower gel?***

*Cheeky bastards!*

***Down your bra. Plenty of room there.***

*Look what happened last time I did that.*

***Never happened before though, yeah.***

*Because I'm careful.*

***Look at it though. Beautiful.***

No fucking stick, not got me stick. Never go shoplifting without it.

***You deserve nice things.***

*I don't need any more L'Occitane, I can hardly get it all under my bed as it is.*

***Limited edition this, though.***

*Just this last one and then I'm stopping.*

**Under her coat it goes.**

She realises she's limping.

***Old.***

Her condition's back.

***Fucked.***

She needs her stick.

***Security guard.***

*What? Where? I can't see him.*

***It's him isn't it.***

*Shit, can't run with my hip like this!*

**Poor little Mandy.**

*Go. Head down. Don't look back.*

**Chicken shit.**

*Fucking leg!*

**Is that his footsteps? He's coming!**

*Throw it away.*

**Rugby-tackled you last time.**

*Should've just put it back!*

**No nice bunch of lads to save ya this time.**

Down the road, round the corner.

**What's he gonna do to ya after last time?**

Hip. Throbbing.

**In front of all these nice people.**

*Fucking shower gel!*

**Watching you get carted off. Oh, hang on a minute…?**

*He's not there is he. He's not even there!*

**Stupid, stupid, bitch!**

*I saw him.*

**Pissed yourself again? Urgh.**

*Wet on my leg.*

**It was funny when you were young.**

*It was definitely him.*

**Disgusting now.**

*Can't move. And now it fucking rains to ruin your hair.*

**Look at yourself, massive mirror on the side of that building, in front of everyone on Market Street, hiding from no one like a dickhead.**

At last she sees herself as she really is.

*Past it.*

Thieving.

*Ill.*

Unhappy.

*Ugly.*

An embarrassment. Cold.

*Cold patch between your legs.*

Mandy just wants to go home now.

*Shitty little flat full of junk.*

*Nice clothes, nice shoes. I've got a lot of nice stuff, me.*

**A hoard of stuff, plucked from the shoplifter's shelf, stashed under the bed.**

*L'Occitane.*

*Greedy, you are. Greedy little bitch.*

*I love L'Occitane.*

*Who the fuck gets obsessed with shower gels?*

At night when she feels empty and alone Mandy sits among neatly ordered boxes of oils and lotions, unscrewing lids – one at a time – to slowly – longingly inhale the magic that makes her feel something she can't put a word to, instead of lonely, scared and fucked…

*Lid off, take it in, nice.*

**It's not gonna be enough.**

Usually it's enough.

**It's not gonna be enough.**

*Sometimes it's enough.*

**It's not gonna be enough.**

*It's not enough.*

**Heroin would be enough.**

*Heroin <u>would</u> be enough.*

**14.**

**The moment he opens his eyes in the hospital, Neil knows things are different.**

He's living proof death can be good for you. When the doctor tells him he died, Neil says,

*Third time lucky, eh.*

The doctor doesn't laugh.

**Next time he wakes up, Mandy's there.**

And when he says,

*I thought I'd never see you again,*

She grabs his face so hard her nails rip his cheek.

**He can't raise his arms to defend himself, it hurts!**

*You fucking dickhead!*

**The nurse comes to ask if everything's alright.**

Mandy doesn't remember doing that.

**Then she puts her head on his chest and even that hurts, but he doesn't say owt.**

*Dickhead!*

**When he wakes up she's gone.**

Later, or the next day, he's not sure which, the doctor's with him when Neil sees Mandy talking to Tattooed Martin through the little window.

**Neil tries to get up but he can't – then he sees her going.** (*To Martin.*) **What did you say to her?**

*You went in me wife's knicker drawer, Neil, that's a big no-no.*

*You went in Mandy's knicker drawer, mate, and she was wearing them at the time!*

*Deflection's a good way to avoid responsibility but I take your point. I tried to warn you but there you go.*

**Warn me about what?**

*She's bad news. When do you get out?*

**They're keeping me in but I'm leaving anyway.**

*You should follow direction for once and don't be a dickhead.*

**As soon as Martin's gone, Neil gets up and demands to be discharged.**

The doctors think, *Fuck it. Free up a bed.* Not in them words.

**There's like this piece of metal running right through him. Unbendable. Hard to describe. He's just feeling it.**

And now he's dressed and ready to go.

**He's made a decision to live and no one can stop him.**

He's never felt anything like it before.

**He strides off the ward with a fist in his chest, *So don't get in the way, yeah?* When he gets to the reception he checks his pockets.**

It's not the first time Neil's had less than a quid to his name.

**47p? *Fuck it, walk.***

He likes walking, always did.

**It feels good to be out, breathing, even though his legs are weak.**

He's even glad his legs are weak, New Neil, because it gives him something to overcome. When he gets to the traffic lights at the top of the hill. He says it out loud,

***I'll walk to fucking Scotland if I have to!***

This woman gives him a look, sidles away, but Neil don't care.

**There's a new voice in his head.**

*This is you now and not one person can tell you what to do!*

**Where the fuck am I though?**

*Who cares, go that way.*

**He doesn't care if he falls over.**

*What are you?*

***I'm a fucking free man!***

*Get to town, get to the hostel, start again.*

***It's a shithole full of junkies.***

*Do it anywhere if you want it.*

***He's feeling the rays of sun on his cheek.***

*All that shit. Flowers, trees, fucking fantastic!*

**He remembers Jesus Christ on Market Street suddenly. Stops dead.**

*Who the fuck <u>was</u> that?*

***I feel sorry for the cunt.***

*You know who it was really.*

***The guy who died. A few days ago. Killed himself. It was me.***

The impressions hitting him are vivid, real. He sees himself before all that.

**Like he is again now.**

That boy.

**He was a good kid. I was a good kid.**

*You were so cheeky.*

**Everyone loved me for it, I felt it back then.**

*Men ruffle your hair, women smile at you.*

**He sees the floor in the kitchen at home. Clear as day. The pattern. The missing tiles. Been there for donkey's them tiles even then.**

*That old lady over the road who gives you biscuits from a tin.*

**His mam's chip pan.**

How broke she always is. Never a thing in the house. *Always made up to see you though.*

**Pang of regret.**

Instant tears in his eyes.

**He wants to go round there now and give her a monster hug like he used to. Wrap her up.**

It always makes her smile that, even when he's bang at it.

**She's so small in his arms. Like a rag doll. Giggles like a girl when he gets hold of her.**

But then he doesn't go round any more. And now it's too late.

**And there it is suddenly.**

He's come some wrong way, stumbled on this view, sprung up in front of him like a giant pop-up picture...

**Manchester.**

The great cityscape sprawling before him.

**Glinting in the sun like the pot of gold at the end of the rainbow.**

There is actually a rainbow.

**Sun shining on Neil, splash of rain bathing Manchester.**

This is the exact moment Mandy stumbles round the corner from Boots and sees herself as she really is in front of everyone on Market Street.

**Neil's leaning on this wall at the top of the hill, looking at the place, glossy and gleaming like he's never seen it before. Another stark pang.**

He's seeing the dead people he knows suddenly.

**His four brothers who ended up on it.**

Got Aids Roger did, but it was the drugs that killed him.

**So many of us. Still dying even now.**

Even Irish Tony ended up on it. It hits him hard now standing there, staring at the city he grew up in. Then a memory.

**Big shop window. Yellow light from the lamp post.**

Boy. He sees it.

**The old city. The one they swept away while he was bang at it.**

And he realises.

*You couldn't get smack back then, it was all just weed and reggae and not even Special Brew yet.*

He thinks,

*We didn't bring it into the country. Not even that twat on the corner selling a bag, looking down his nose at us did that.*

He sees himself in jail again.

*That scouse lad on the Kitchens said it. Wonder what happened to him…?*

*One minute we've taken Liverpool, next minute I'm jumping over the counter at the offie with an Uzi tryna feed an habit.*

*Maggie Thatcher's brown, they called it in there.*

He remembers the relief of jail…

**Once he's done his rattle it's a break in there. Get down the gym. Bulk up.**

Get out looking fit.

**Then bang at it again. He's angry now, kicking the wall.**

He doesn't know the actual facts of the political history Neil,

**The full extent of it.**

That before the riots in eighty-one there's three thousand heroin addicts in the whole of Britain – mostly middle class.

**Four years later there's three hundred and thirty thousand – nearly all of them working class. Ten thousand in Manchester alone.**

He doesn't know about William Whitelaw and the reports and all that.

**The important cops and military brass sitting round polished tables talking about them.**

He doesn't know about the decision they take, these people, not to bust the biggest dealers, even though everyone of them's known from Liverpool to Kabul.

**Neil doesn't know the new head of the army they appoint after the riots specialises in psychological warfare and nurturing criminal gangs.**

That he's accused of war crimes now in Ireland and Kenya, this general.

**That he says in a book he writes on crushing rebellion:**

*When push comes to shove 'the law becomes a propaganda cover for the disposal of unwanted members of the public'.*

**Neil doesn't know they use the heroin crime wave to give the police massive new powers,**

For the disposal of unwanted members of the public...?

**He doesn't know the British, French and American military have been working with the biggest drugs cartels in the world for decades:**

French Connection,

**Golden Triangle,**

Afghanistan, Colombia – smack and crack:

**They're up to their ears in it.**

He knows fuck-all about any of them details, Neil.

**But when the only place you feel free's in jail, you don't need a history lesson.**

It's in your blood.

**He's glaring at Manchester now, feeling it rising up: this rage – choking him.**

His eye trips on something.

**The blot on the horizon.**

Right there in the middle of it all, staring Manchester down like some bastard overseer.

**The dirty brown tower of Strangeways nick.**

Massive middle finger to the likes of Neil that tower.

**Haunting the city since the days of Engles and Queen Victoria.**

Everyone in there on something, or selling it. *Remember when they burned it down?*

**1st of April 1990.**

*We weren't the fools that day, eh.*

**Neil sees himself, heart singing, marching down there to cheer the lads on the roof. Ripped the place to shreds, they did.**

What a feeling, seeing them all up there, on the smashed-up roof like that.

**Broken, smoking shell of F wing.**

Still smouldering it is when Neil gets there.

*Beautiful.* **Standing there in the morning sun, staring at the sight.**

By twelve there's ten of his old mates there, half an hour later fifteen, sixteen seventeen, more on the way.

*What a buzz.*

Junkies of Manchester gathered for a jamboree.

**Playing Spot-the-Prisoner-on-the-Roof.**

*Int that David Long, look, next to the kid with the banner.*

**Fucking hell and there's Simmo.**

*That twat grassed me up last year, the snake!*

*(Together.)* **Yo, Simmo!!** / *Yo Simmo!*

*(Both salute Simmo with fists raised.)*

**Then we see him, standing there a few feet away.**

*Can't be!*

*It's not is it? Where's his security?*

*Fucking is!*

**They can't believe their eyes.**

Ragamuffin army of pale-faced skeletons, indoor eyes blinking in the daylight at the sight.

*It's <u>him</u>!*

Stood there on a wall, he is, so everyone can get a look.

**TV cameras pointing at him.**

*No Mufti squad? Nerve of the guy!*

*It's Governor fucking O'Friel!*

Bastard in charge of the burning nick. Talking to the news like he's just some guy in a suit.

**We're all looking around suddenly aware of something big.**

Hardly a uniform in sight. *How many of us are there?*

*Enough!* **The times they've hated him!**

Up on a charge, some shit a screw throws at you.

**Marched down the block for the night.**

Next day up in front of one of O'Friel's minions. Don't even look up some of 'em.

**Bang. Loss of remission. Days added on, months sometimes, over and over…**

Genuine dictatorship in the heart of Manchester.

*We can have him!*

*Right here, right now, in front of the burnt-out shell of his own fucking nick!*

*Do it for the lads on the roof!*

But they're feeling it now, the whole lot of them.

**That old feeling, pit of the stomach. The need to score.**

(*Sudden change of heart.*) *Probly hiding though, int they.*

*Van of the bastards somewhere, waiting for us to make a move.*

And we're gone.

**Gang of junkies marching down the road to score together.**

Laughing for once. Talking about the lads on the roof.

**Back in the now, legs wobbling beneath him, leaning on the wall looking over the view of the city, Neil feels a pang of shame.**

Dirty brown tower in the distance. He thinks,

*We let them down that day, the lads.*

But then some office window in the distance catches the sun and flashes him a wink.

**And he has to admit it.**

The glass and steel. The shiny, new city…

*It looks fucking epic from here.*

And he knows suddenly. He gets it, clear as day.

**A generation of junkies, for a mountain of shining junk.**

*The bastards!*

**He jumps up suddenly.**

*New start now, yeah.*

***I'm still fucking here.***

He's feeling it again, the steel inside. Unbendable.

***Next time I'll be right. Next time I'll be ready.***

**15.**

**He gets a job, Neil does.**

*No way!*

**Gets into a better hostel, does voluntary work, gets a placement working with offenders.**

He's well qualified there.

**And then he gets this chance for a proper job, salary and all that.**

How long does that take?

**Two years.**

Shit. What about Mandy?

**The job's in this posh building in the Northern Quarter…**

Oh.

**He walks everywhere these days, Neil does. And he's there in the Northern Quarter, on his way to the interview…**

Is it two years since they've seen each other?

**Yeah, but it's not so much the length of time…**

She sees him coming, Mandy does, tries to dodge behind the old post office, but,

*Mandy!*

She knows how she looks, but she brazens it out.

**Tries to anyhow.**

Fucking stick, she's trying not to lean on it. *Neil! Fucking state of you, man. What's the matter with ya!*

**He's wearing a suit.**

*You think you're Prince Charles now, or what?*

**It's a shock. Neil tries not to show it, but. Two more years of heroin has ruined her.**

Her hip's bad, it makes it look worse than it is. She's having a bad day.

**There's a smell about her. Neil tries not to notice it. Does a good job. It comes back to him later.**

*My hip's bad,* she says. *I'm having a bad day.*

*I've got an interview in there,* he says.

*Fuckin hell. Someone's giving you a job?*

**Tell me about it.**

*Let me guess, drug worker?*

**It's great to think there's a job out there that I'm the most qualified person for.**

*Lend me a tenner, Neil.*

**What?**

*Come on, I'm having a bad day.*

**So you said.**

*Some dickhead robbed my purse and I'm on my period, I need tampons.*

**I haven't actually got a tenner.**

*There's a cash point round the corner, come on, you've got a card ant ya, you must have looking like that.*

**I've got a card but they're waiting for me in there.**

*Who is, they can wait five minutes can't they?*

**It's an interview, Mandy.**

*Well give me your card, I'll get it myself, bring it back in a minute, get what I need, leave it with someone. What's wrong, don't you trust me?*

*Sorry, Mandy.*

*Why you being tight? Why you being a twat about it? You think I wouldn't do the same for you if I had it and you didn't. I thought you were alright, Neil. Forget it then… (Going.)*

**Mandy, wait. He doesn't want to leave it like that.**

He's thinking about giving her his card, she can tell.

*Just… wait a minute.*

*I've always had a soft spot for you, Neil, you know I have. Tell you what, do your interview, we'll go for a drink after, or a coffee or whatever you drink now, and tonight we can go somewhere and have a good time, yeah, just the two of us. Gimme your card, I'll wait for you –*

Then she realises. His face. He's trying not to cry.

**You know what, fuck the interview, I'll take you to a meeting, come on.**

*Meeting? No! I'm alright, what you on about?*

**What time is it? Come for a coffee, we can go somewhere and talk.**

*Look. Forget it. I'm sorry. Get in there, go on, you deserve summat nice. You look the part. You look good. You really do.*

**Why don't you wait? I won't be long.**

*No. It's not for everyone. Go. And good luck. Go!*

**And she turns and she walks away. Just like that.**

It looks worse than it is.

**He watches her go. This little figure, disappearing into the well-dressed throng.**

Stick making a stick noise.

**16.**

**A couple of months later Neil's just finished sharing at a meeting.**

Giving it all that, like he does: 'Stark bollock naked on Market Street', 'I've died three times, me', 'If I can get clean anyone can'. People look up to him for it.

**There's a newcomer there, Neil's hoping the lad's gonna get it. It's like, when someone's at their first meeting, your life depends on saying something that'll catch them...**

The door opens. Mandy walks in.

**Shuffles over to a seat. Head down.**

Sits there with this look on her face. Defeat.

**She won't look at anyone. Refuses to look at anyone.**

She doesn't want to see the judgement on their faces.

**But not a single one of them is judging her. Everyone in the room's rooting for her. Eventually, after a lot of shuffling in his seat and waggling his head, Mandy relents and Neil catches her eye and smiles.**

She tries to smile back, but it's more like... *Fuck off! Twat.*

**Narcotics and Counter-revolution**
*Postscript to* The Political History of Smack and Crack

The real political history of smack and crack has very little to do with the attitude of one British parliamentary party or another, or the doings of some particular Home Secretary during the brief time he or she is allowed to handle a lever or two of state power.

They have a lot to say about narcotics, these people, and write a lot of white papers allegedly to deal with the tsunami of hard drugs that floods Britain from just after the time Margaret Thatcher wins her famous landslide in 1979, when 27% of the electorate vote for her, the moment modern British history begins to really take shape.

Decades of chaos and ruin follow as the hard-drug epidemic spreads in tandem with what is known as 'Thatcherism', but which is more properly called 'neo-liberal economic policy', as it rips through working-class districts, tearing the old communities apart, helping reshape them in the new mould.

As the narcotics take hold, parliamentarians of all colours huff with indignation, boil with anger, or voice concern for the victims of the accompanying crime wave – and even occasionally for some of the addicts. But they pass ever more laws to make criminals of the victims of the disaster, massively increase police powers of all kinds – supposedly to deal with the accompanying crime wave – and wake up too late to the Aids and hepatitis epidemics exacerbated by the very criminal culture they help to create.

Never do British parliamentarians seem able or willing to grasp the bigger picture, or even realise there might be one.

To relate the history of the politics of hard drugs within the framework of British parliamentary practice hobbles the story completely. From the point of view of smack and crack, it hardly counts as politics at all, being more of a reaction *to* the politics – a distraction or a distorting element, an aggravating factor, but mostly an irrelevance.

My play *The Political History of Smack and Crack* highlights only one of the main aspects of the real political history: its emergence in the wake of Thatcherism and in particular of the 1981 inner-city uprisings. But in the end a play has to follow its characters and operate within the laws of dramatic structure/entertainment. I tried in earlier drafts to include more of the international background but when we tried it out on a variety of audiences – from semi-professional boxers in Barnsley, to students in Bolton and recovering addicts in Manchester – the feeling was that while these details are very interesting they are too difficult to grasp during the play itself and anyway a distraction from the main thrust of Neil and Mandy's story.

So what follows is a brief summary of the international story, which is covered elsewhere by historians in more detail, but which vastly reinforces the message of the play when you take it all as a whole.

It all comes from respectable public sources – US congressional hearings, declassified government documents, carefully researched academic writing, etc. And there's a short must-read list at the end if you want to know more, or do some in depth fact-checking.

## The Prehistory

The prehistory of the modern narcotic trade runs through different eras, beginning in earnest with the Opium Wars against China. In the 1870s, Queen Victoria's navy ruthlessly oversee the birth of the greatest opium addiction epidemic in history for the purposes of oiling the wheels of commerce and Empire, which go together like a toot of heroin and a hit on the crack pipe.

For details of how the Chinese opium epidemic of the late 1800s and early 1900s is later completely eradicated, see the 1949 communist revolution, touched on below.

Heroin itself is only invented and produced on an industrial scale in the 1870s by the German corporation that also gives us Germolene. The new wonder drug is originally marketed as a non-addictive alternative to opium, but then again Bayer Corporation also use and kill Jewish prisoners from Auschwitz in medical experiments during the Nazi period, so what do you expect from a company like that.[1]

From here the history of heroin appears as an insane kaleidoscope of colourfully villainous characters and tangled plots spanning the globe, dazzling in its daring, shocking in its depravity. See the Mafia, the French Connection, the Golden Triangle, the Vietnam War, the carnage in Colombia, the war in Afghanistan and more recently the almost total collapse of Mexican towns and cities. But buried in this apparently chaotic and anarchic narrative are ragged but distinct through-lines of meaning, waiting to be unearthed like themes in a Beckett play.

In truth, as we shall see here, history shows that since World War II the international narcotics trade has been blood brother to the politics of counter-revolution – 'counter-subversion', or 'counter-insurgency' to them – a tool in the desperate struggle of the world's capitalist powers to prevail at all costs in the face of equally desperate resistance.

## The Birth of the Modern Mafia

Bayer Corporation's pharmaceutical heroin of the late 1800s and early 1900s isn't yet the smack of Neil and Mandy's story, but the accompanying shenanigans does begin to sketch a rough early draft of the script.

Many private disasters are undoubtedly spawned by Bayer Corps' ruthless mismarketing of the super-addictive new substance, but the tragedy only becomes political in 1920 with Prohibition, the complete banning of alcohol sales in the USA, which gives heroin a double boost.

During Prohibition, consumption of pharmaceutical heroin is an obvious alcohol substitute and this want-satisfaction creates for the first time a wider market for heroin, and encourages the beginnings of an organised illegal trade within the USA.

At this point in the US there is no access to independently manufactured heroin. Supply is mostly stolen from corporate laboratories, with many a willing addicted worker helping in what soon becomes industrial-scale theft.

In the early 1930s the looming end of Prohibition suddenly creates for the first time a climate of insecurity among the younger generation of Mafia bootleggers and illegal alcohol distributers, giving heroin its second big boost.[2]

A shooting war breaks out between, on the one side, forces supporting the already rich, socially conservative and therefore more anti-drug generation of gangsters – personified by Al Capone – and on the other, the pro-narcotic young guns running day-to-day bootlegging and distribution networks, yet to make their fortunes. Without the lucrative trade in illicit alcohol, the young guns face reduced prospects of maintaining themselves in the style to which they have become accustomed in the post-Wall Street-crash economic climate. Out of this colourful maelstrom, loosely illustrated by a new generation of film-makers and actors, such as Cecil B. DeMille and Edward G. Robinson, emerges a new and ruthlessly well-organised Mafia.[3]

The necessities of this armed, intergenerational struggle dictate new, tightly bound forms of organisation, inspired by, but exceeding in scale, the traditional methods of organisation imported from Sicily where, however, the new Mafia still has strong ties. By the end of 1931, a new leader has emerged to consolidate the first, modern, fully national crime/business syndicate: Lucky Luciano. The central body of this organisation is known as 'The Commission', which has its own armed wing known as 'Murder Incorporated' – holy muse to many a black-and-white movie-maker. So now Mafia scores and disputes are settled nationally, staving off future gang wars and enabling the smooth running of core businesses – gambling, prostitution and now heroin.[4]

But gambling quickly hits economic limits. Prostitutes, forced to live by wit and guile, are often ungovernable and are understandably prone to stealing what is, after all, their own income, especially when they discover heroin. Heroin itself soon proves the most reliable and profitable modern Mafia business; it's the perfect capitalist commodity, demand magically expanding with supply.[5]

## The Death of the Modern Mafia

By the mid-1930s a Mafia/US government synergy has emerged, evidenced by the well-documented state-sponsored use of Mafia violence against trade-union, working-class and other political activists.[6] But with the rise of fascism in Europe and the looming prospect of a world war, it seems the FBI has become concerned about the demoralising spread of heroin among the poorer communities and the impact of gangsterism on popular morale which may undermine a future war effort. Anyway, a highly effective nationwide campaign of intimidation and imprisonment is mounted by the Federal authorities against their former, unofficial allies. In a few short years the supposedly indestructible national organisation of the modern Mafia is crushed almost completely.

By 1936, Lucky Luciano has gone from a celebrated public figure, invited to all the fanciest New York parties where he rubs shoulders with the rich, the glamorous and the powerful, to Sing Sing's most notorious prisoner, serving thirty to fifty years.[7]

Enter Mussolini.

During the consolidation of fascist power in Italy, the Sicilian Mafia make a near-fatal miscalculation and meet a fate similar to that of their US counterpart.

Legend has it that the Sicilian leadership sees the new Roman Emperor as a rude upstart – perhaps understandable considering Mafia sway on the Island of Sicily stretches back centuries. When 'Il Duce' visits Sicily, local Mafia bosses demonstrate their power by calling for a boycott of Mussolini's public speeches. Meeting everywhere with empty plazas, the duly insulted Emperor carries out a demonstration of his own: with a fully modern, newly acquired state power behind him, and the new national vehemence at his side, Mussolini quickly and ruthlessly crushes what is essentially a primitive, Sicilian-clan hangover. Using fascist muscle and all the finery of a state machine, the new Emperor dispatches those Mafiosi who escape the bullet and the torture chamber back to the hills to continue their time-honoured tradition of goat farming.[8]

It's a colourful tale, but whatever the true detail, the outcome is the same: Mussolini all but destroys the organisation of the Italian Mafia in Sicily, where defeated Mafiosi burn with hatred for the new Emperor.[9]

### The Resurrection of the Modern Mafia

With war comes revolution.

At home during the war, US authorities witness an alarming upswing in radical industrial activity and grass-roots agitation. Abroad, following Hitler's defeat at Stalingrad in 1943, the battle-hardened Soviet Red Army sweeps across Europe towards Berlin, bringing in its wake, as far as US Army generals are concerned, the threat of a communist takeover of the whole of ruined Europe.[10]

Add to this the anti-capitalist feeling among many European resistance leaders who have witnessed the majority of their national leaders capitulate to, or collaborate with, fascism. There must be a suspicion too among these fighters that US and British Empire generals have scrambled round Africa defending their colonies only to join the real fray when a German defeat looks inevitable, while the Soviets have fought and died by the million confronting Nazi Germany head-on.

The US government's immediate tasks in the climax and resolution of World War II then are to discipline labour at home and prevent an anti-capitalist takeover in Europe. The Italian Mafia answer their prayers twice over.

During the war at the New York dockyards, the problem of industrial unrest is compounded by another urgent issue of national security: the passing of shipping information to the German naval high command by Italian seamen and dock-workers leading to increased loss of allied tonnage at sea. There is even rumoured to be secret offshore fuelling of German U-boats.[11]

Meanwhile on the Island of Sicily, political, geographical and military factors combine to create the perfect circumstances for a softer US invasion of, as they see it, communist-threatened Europe.

Enter the much-maligned Lt Commander Haffenden of the US Navy, whose family dispute the meaning of the well-documented facts to this day.

Despite the pre-war FBI crackdown, small-time New York Mafiosi have managed to keep a foothold in illegal racketeering at the New York docks. Alerted to this, Lt Commander Haffenden initiates secret contact with Boss of Bosses Lucky Luciano in Sing Sing through a dockland mobster named Socks Lanza.[12]

A series of intricate negotiations take place in which Luciano agrees to use his dockland influence to crush strikes and oppose pro-German activity on the waterfront. More significantly, Luciano also agrees to aid a US invasion of Sicily where anti-Mussolini feeling can easily be harnessed to give US armed forces a helping hand. In exchange, the US government agrees to commute the remainder of Lucky Luciano's sentence at end of the war.[13]

Another legend has it that the US army has in its possession, during the successful 1943 invasion of Sicily, a yellow silk scarf embroidered with the letter 'L', given to them by the Boss of Bosses as a token of his blessing for the venture. Whatever the truth of the detail, as a result of a very real Luciano deal, the US military get Mafia spies, Mafia guides and a Mafia-inspired uprising to help them on their way to Berlin, via a softly yielding Italy, from a secure base in Sicily.[14]

In return, at the end of World War II, the US installs Mafia mayors in every town in Sicily,[15] from where the mobsters lead the charge in the whole of southern Italy against the organisations of the working class that have fought Mussolini and are now demanding a voice in government – and in many cases calling for the overthrow of capitalism.

Back in the US, the government keeps its promises to their man in Sing Sing. The newly emboldened Mafia take over the running of selected labour unions, especially those 'on the waterfront': cue Marlon Brando. Meanwhile, Lucky Luciano is released but deported to Sicily, from which hallowed ground the returning hero goes on during the late 1940s and 1950s to lay the foundations of the modern international heroin trade.[16]

## The French Connection

Such perverse synergy between gangsters and state – a necessary prerequisite for drug-dealing on any internationally significant scale – is evident in other parts of Europe at the climax and resolution of World War II.

In Germany not so much. Here gangsters help run the concentration camps but only as privileged and ruthless prisoner/overseers, and many eventually perish there themselves as their organisations have done before them at the hands of the Nazis.[17] Popular German resistance to Nazism is largely destroyed before the outbreak of war.

Here the US military is struggling against an outside force: the Soviets in the east of the country. This they manage reasonably well without gangsterism, in part by keeping the ex-Nazi state's chief of military intelligence in the east in post to conduct anti-Soviet activity[18] – whilst also, lest we forget, helping ex-Gestapo officers escape to South America where they will become stalwarts of US-backed fascist regimes for decades to come.[19]

In France, post-war state/gangster collusion is the twin of that in Italy, but here the US military intelligence pact is with the Corsican Mafia. The Corsican Mafia is to France what the Sicilian Mafia is to Italy, with similar Mediterranean-island clan origins and ruthlessly violent traditions. But whereas the Sicilian Mafia have a rigid vertical structure, the Corsicans have traditionally worked in close-knit but separate cells capable of working in concert but operationally independent, much like the units of a modern guerrilla army. Plus, neither Marlon Brando, Al Pacino, nor any other Hollywood A-list celebrity has ever portrayed a Corsican Mafiosi, and outside of Southern Europe and the French colonial world their fame has burned dimly.

In France, the post-war power struggle between revolutionary forces and the old order is a close-run thing, especially in Marseilles. The old southern sea port is the national capital of the French Resistance, where many of its best fighters are drawn from the city's radical dock-workers. During the war itself the Resistance gets much-needed assistance in the form of arms and people-smuggling from the anti-Nazi Corsican Mafia, who are good at that stuff.[20]

At the end of the war, with the collaborationist southern French (Vichy) government discredited, communist-led Resistance forces even manage to secure control of several departments of the Marseilles police force, including the CID. Meanwhile, the Corsican Mafia are approached by US military intelligence and offered protection (and weapons and cash) in return for a campaign of intimidation against their former Resistance comrades, particularly any communists.[21] The Mafiosi oblige and several striking workers are brutally murdered. In a countermove, staunch comrades of the Marseilles CID launch a highly effective police campaign against the criminal activities of the Corsican Mafia, namely gambling, prostitution and narcotics.[22]

But capitalist-friendly police units, especially the crack riot police previously used by the collaborationist Vichy regime to carry out orders from Nazi Germany – including deportations to the concentration camps – are mobilised to swing the balance of power in favour of the old order. Soon the radical remnants of the heroic French Resistance are smashed, the police force is purged of communists and the Marseilles CID goes back to its time-honoured incompetence and blind-eye-turning to the Corsican underworld.[23]

Politically, the matter is settled by the newly elected, larger-than-life millionaire socialist mayor of Marseilles, Gaston Defferre. A hero of the wartime underground, respected by all for his wartime association with the Resistance, Defferre decisively sides with the old order. By the time the communists are ousted from the police and working-class activists are dead, dispersed or disheartened, Defferre has the two most notorious Corsican gangsters – the brothers Guerini – for his personal bodyguards.[24]

From here, the Corsican Mafia use the post-war political protection granted them to establish a network of laboratories in the city of Marseilles to refine imported raw opium into heroin. The famous French Connection is, in fact, the crime-child of US military intelligence, anti-communist French authorities and the Corsican Mafia.[25]

Enter Gene Hackman, ace detective in his pork-pie hat, to not discover any of this.

In the early 1950s raw opium is sourced internationally by Lucky Luciano's Italian Mafia and transported to France, where it is refined by Corsican Mafiosi. From here it is transported to the USA, mostly by the Italians. It is met at the New York docks by criminal networks re-established in the US during the wartime struggle against dockside labour militancy.[26]

The resolution of World War II thus sees a spectacular return for Lucky Luciano and the US Mafia, and a political coup for their neighbours in Corsica – who are soon sourcing raw opium themselves directly from the French military in Vietnam where, as we will see, Lucky Luciano's Mafia will eventually play their part too.


**The Road to 'Nam**

The harrowing picture anti-capitalist Europe presents to capitalist HQ in 1945 is nothing compared to the vision of hell it faces in the soon-to-be-ex-colonies of Asia, where millions are up in arms and making rapid headway towards self-government.

Gangsterism to the rescue once again.

First up: the French in Vietnam. Or as it is known at the time, 'French Indochina'.

In 1946, inspired by the revolutionary leadership of Ho Chi Minh and enraged by 100 years of plunder and cruelty by occupying foreign powers, the people of what will become Vietnam rise up against French colonial rule. Meanwhile, incompetent (or arrogant) French generals who have made their names during World War II simply don't understand the form of revolutionary warfare they now face. These generals see the country as a series of empty spaces in which to conduct flaking movements or great sweeps, as they might against an army like that of the recently defeated Japanese. But the Asian revolutionaries of the 1940s and 1950s by now understand that the best way to beat the militarily superior forces of an occupying power is to merge as far as possible with the people themselves and take advantage of their massively superior numbers.

The decisive revolutionary strategy of the day therefore is to unite the population in what Fidel Castro will later call a 'total war of all the people'.

By 1950, after four years of bitter counter-revolutionary fighting, during which the French war effort has become ever more unpopular back home in France, younger, more forward-thinking French generals realise the old tactics are losing the war. These innovative military thinkers concoct a wonderfully depraved scheme – soon to be mirrored by the CIA in the mountains of Burma and shortly after by the British in Kenya – that will by the 1980s become the new normal for the international counter-revolution.[27]

Instead of designing grand classical manoeuvres, the younger French generals realise a political strategy is required to accompany the military action. Led by General Roger Trinquier, enterprising and independent French intelligence units embark on a strategy to divide the population against itself so that a 'total war of all the people' will be difficult to organise. These units correctly conceive the country as an intricate network of interconnected villages containing complex, often archaic social structures in which there may be tribal, religious, or other primitive authorities, such as a local warlord, that might fear or resent the prospect of the socialist future promised the poor masses by Ho Chi Minh's revolutionaries.[28]

Soon there is a network of forty thousand warlords, medieval-hangovers, misfits, bandits, crackpots, religious fanatics and assorted malcontents, armed and organised into despotic militia and spy networks friendly to French colonial rule. Many of these fiefdoms do indeed become difficult or impossible for the revolutionaries to penetrate but – and here's the rub – they cost big dollar. To set up a band of 150 men in the 1950s with basic training, weapons and bonuses, the cost in today's terms would be $130,000. For forty thousand souls therefore you're looking at $35 million in today's money just to get them off the ground. Bands must then be granted annual stipends of up to the equivalent of $750,000 in today's money and continually armed and maintained as viable units, provided with cash for bribes, etc. And realistically forty thousand men is just a start.[29]

In early 1950s Vietnam this strategy does begin to show promise for the French, but how to pay the bill? Because of the unpopularity of the war at home, the French National Assembly has reduced its outlay to regular military units to an absolute minimum. And anyway these units are under the control of the gallant-pose-striking gentlemen generals of the old guard who see Trinquier and his comrades as rude and reckless upstarts. In the end hardly a franc or a dollar is forthcoming for the young generals' promising counter-revolutionary scheme.

The solution is the poetically named Operation X. Otherwise known as drug-dealing on an industrial scale.

From the days of Queen Victoria's Opium Wars through to as recently as the 1950s, many of the monarchies and republics of South and Southeast Asia have operated one form or another of official monopoly in the opium trade. This highly lucrative system of supply to and taxation of the millions of opium-smokers from Hong Kong to Saigon is usually conducted by some combination of official authority in the particular country. For instance, for many decades of the early 1900s, the Thai Royal family derive a significant portion of their fortune from the business.[30] Seen as everything from a free lunch to a necessary evil in the region itself, the trade is the epitome of moral degradation to respectable governments in the imperial centres who see themselves as the civilising element of world history. The projection of this high-minded moral appearance is all the more important in Asia in the wake of World War II, with communist bastards everywhere promising free universal health care, shelter and education to the wretched of the Earth.

So when, in the early 1950s, wholesome western diplomats begin persuading the majority of Asian authorities to declare the opium trade illegal, our swashbuckling French pioneer generals in Vietnam see a golden opportunity. In practice, the region-wide decrees outlawing narcotics make little difference to Asian opium eaters and smokers themselves, nor to the scale of the overall trade, but they do gift one of the world's great sources of profit to gangsters. The biggest and baddest of these gangsters in Vietnam soon turn out to be secret units of the intelligence department of the French Expeditionary Corps.[31]

By 1951, French army general Roger Trinquier, mastermind of Operation X, has become godfather to the greatest illegal narcotics smuggling network the modern world has so far seen.

Under the watchful eye of dynamic young generals, French military aircraft fly tons of raw opium from the poppy fields of Laos to be sold in Saigon to gangsters protected by corrupt Vietnamese police and customs officers, themselves protected by secret elements of the French and Vietnamese military. The profits then pay handsomely for the Trinquier-inspired counter-revolutionary gangs. Some of this opium also finds its way to heroin refineries in Marseilles, courtesy of Corsican Mafiosi, where it strengthens the hand of the anti-radical alliance in the south of France. At the same time, and also in Marseilles, radical dock-workers are striking in support of the Vietnamese independence struggle, while themselves under attack from ex-Vichy riot police and murderous heroin-smuggling Corsican gangsters.[32]

Thus heroin creates a truly international counter-revolutionary symbiosis.

Though victorious against the working class of Marseilles, the counter-revolution in Vietnam is ultimately thwarted. The Vietnamese people's fighting spirit is too strong. The power of the generals of the French military old guard is too entrenched and the old generals themselves are too arrogant to adapt to the new circumstances. And, anyway, the brutality and corruption of the misfit militias funded by Operation X eventually begins to alienate the populations of the disputed areas. It all comes to a head in 1954 with the massive destruction of French forces at the Battle of Dien Bien Phu, which brings to a close one hundred years of French colonial rule in Indochina.

In the wake of this great victory – or defeat, depending on how you view it – the north of Vietnam is taken over by a revolutionary government determined to spread their revolution to the whole country. In the south, the French reluctantly hand over power to the USA. Over the next few years the US military establish a puppet government and pretend newly created South Vietnam is an independent country.[33] Meanwhile, US Mafiosi move in alongside the US authorities to assist in the drug-dealing.[34]

By the late 1950s/early 1960s, control of the Saigon-centred opium/heroin network of warlords, gangsters and armed religious fanatics established under the French has become the political and military key to holding the whole of South Vietnam.[35] By this time too, a tropical cyclone of drug money has swept into the furthest corners of the Southern Vietnamese civil and political system and set it to rot. Propping up such a corrupt political entity proves an impossible feat that 57,000 US soldiers will nonetheless die trying to achieve, in what becomes famous as the Vietnam War, or 'Nam to its friends.

*INTERESTING LINK: French godfather-general Roger Trinquier is today considered a leading light of western counter-revolutionary warfare theory. Trinquier's military writings are admired and quoted at length and used as a template by the best-known British army counter-revolutionary theorist General Sir Frank Kitson.[36] Kitson is the man appointed by the Thatcher government to direct UK mainland forces in the wake of the 1981 inner-city uprisings depicted in this play.*

## The Golden Triangle

In the late 1940s and early 1950s, while the French are getting their pounding in Vietnam, the US has its own headache next door in the form of the Chinese revolution, for which it prescribes the same painkiller.

In 1949, to quote the great chronicler of the event, Edgar Snow, 'The Chinese revolution breaks onto the international stage with all the force of a nuclear explosion.'[37] As a result of the revolution, the collapsed Chinese regime of butchers and buriers-of-people-alive, quasi-medieval warlords and their henchmen and hangers-on, plus the ragged remains of the defeated and hated, western-backed Kuomintang army, drag their sorry remains out of the country to colonise the rugged, poppy-growing mountains of neighbouring Burma. Here they dream of bloody revenge and plot the re-conquest of China.

From the US perspective, the situation facing world capitalism now surely appears critical. Soviet forces are ensconced in Eastern Europe, the Chinese revolution has mobilised a fifth of the world's population, revolutionary war has erupted in Vietnam and is spilling into the neighbouring mountains of Burma, Laos and Cambodia. Building counter-revolutionary forces in the region is top priority. However, sending US troops to fight inside China will only fan the flames of revolution, as the French are already finding in Vietnam. So the urgent tasks of stopping the spread of revolution and taking back China fall to the clandestine intelligence organisations (through this very process becoming the CIA we know today),[38] who have to conduct these operations in secret using covert forces, otherwise known as mercenaries.

The dynamics of this process are best explained by the rugged warrior-scholar of the world heroin trade, Alfred McCoy. In the early 1960s, McCoy pulls up his bootstraps and climbs the Burmese mountains to discover the truth of what is going on from the warlords and poppy-growing tribespeople themselves. Later McCoy interviews most of the big players in the French military and the Vietnamese and Laotian narcotic smuggling gangs – including French godfather-general Roger Trinquier himself – most of whom are perfectly frank about their activities. Today McCoy is considered the world's leading authority on the subject.

McCoy:

> By drawing on the resources of a powerful tribal leader or local warlord, a CIA agent could achieve a covert operational capacity far beyond his budget limits... In a region of weak microstates and fragmented tribes, such strongmen usually combined traditional authority with control over the local

economy. In the Golden Triangle, the only commodity was opium and the most powerful local leaders were the opium warlords.[39]

As one such CIA-backed warlord, General Tuan Shi-wen, himself tells McCoy: 'To fight you must have an army, and an army must have guns, and to buy guns you must have money. In these mountains the only money is opium.'

McCoy again:

> This interplay among opium, money, and political power drew the CIA into a complicitous relationship with the Golden Triangle drug trade. In its covert warfare, the CIA's strength was no more or less than that of its local clients. To maintain the power that mobilised tribal armies and marched them into battle, these warlords used the CIA's resources – arms, ammunition, and, above all, air transport – to increase their control over the opium crop.[40]

By the time the CIA fully take over French operations in Vietnam in 1954–6, after the French defeat at Dien Bien Phu, the whole narcotic trade of Burma, Laos, Vietnam and Thailand has become one hugely profitable international counter-revolutionary effort. But with illegal narcotics, of course, come violence and corruption, which in turn create political chaos, not to mention scandal. The details of each internationally embarrassing bust or public outrage differ, and many an official head rolls – to be quickly replaced by another – but essentially the narcotic trade of the late 1950s and 1960s (and the first half of the 1970s) remains the same. The main beneficiaries remain the same also: whoever is helping the CIA against the revolutions in China and Vietnam.

Eventually, the re-invasion of China, using such ill-disciplined and corrupt warlords in tandem with the discredited old regime, fails, as does the covert effort to stop the Vietnamese revolution crossing the mountain borders of the surrounding nations. After this – from about 1965 – the US military sends its own troops to die in their tens of thousands in Vietnam while their B-52s famously carpet-bomb the region, using more explosive power than is used during the whole of World War II by all sides.[41]

At its height, the military situation in 'Nam is absurdly macabre. For example, as the largest contingents of US troops begin to arrive on the ground from 1965 onwards, Vietnamese generals (aided by US Mafiosi) peddle enormous quantities of the purest heroin to tens of thousands of the very GIs who have come to save them.[42] By the famous Fall of Saigon in 1975, the military situation is so chaotic and the political situation so utterly corrupt that neither the CIA nor the US military high command can properly discover what is happening on the ground to their own forces. The fog of war is by then as impenetrable as the mind of a heroin addict who's just had a hit. (See Robert McNamara interviewed in the film *The Fog of War*.)

This brief characterisation of French and US state-sponsored drug-dealing from the 1950s to the 1970s is, of course, vastly oversimplified and the realities are far more complex and nuanced – and often more interesting and even more depraved. But it is accurate. Obviously not everyone in the US military is aware of what the CIA or the secret units of the French military are doing in the Golden Triangle in terms of drug-dealing, and very few in the US and French governments back home in the West have a clue. But it is clear from the records that anyone who does discover the truth either keeps shtum for the sake of the war effort, or is silenced by those they report to. But for anyone who wants to see it, the evidence is clear.

Over the period of their involvement in Vietnam, the US military and even the South Vietnamese government itself do make attempts to curtail the heroin trade, especially when it threatens to completely derail the war effort. Many of these anti-drug drives are half-hearted and nominal, but some of them are serious, full-blooded and use every device from the judiciary to targeted assassination. Some of the measures even temporarily succeed.[43] Ultimately, though, they all fail as spectacularly as US political and military strategy itself. The vast American forces and their supporters are eventually defeated in the greatest military humiliation in history, inflicted by the poor but determined people of a small country.

By 1975, two million Vietnamese people have died fighting and 57,000 American soldiers have died defending a hopelessly corrupt narco-state.

## From Vietnam to Moss Side

Especially from a Western perspective, everything so far
described is small beans compared to the CIA-sponsored
narcotic trade of the 1980s, which is centred on the counter-
revolutionary gangs of the Afghan mujahideen and the
Nicaraguan contras (who link directly to the Colombian cartels
made famous by Pablo Escobar).[44]

In the 1950s, 1960s and early 1970s, despite the best efforts of
New York, Sicilian and Corsican Mafiosi, the vast majority of
the opium and heroin from the Golden Triangle is consumed in
Asia itself. There are some significant outbreaks of heroin
addiction in the USA, particularly in Chicago and New York –
traditional Mafia strongholds – mostly around the time of the
civil rights movement. But compared to the US and European
drug epidemics of the 1980s, the numbers are insignificant.
From the Western point of view, the Reagan/Thatcher foreign-
policy era is like the Golden Triangle on crack.

But although, again from the Western point of view, the scale of
the drug-dealing associated with the counter-revolutionary
efforts of the 1980s is different, the patterns are almost
identical. The morals, motives and methods seem to have been
transplanted directly from the past to the present.

To pluck out a few grubby details of the story for those who can
still bear to look:

Over the decade of US covert military involvement in
Afghanistan, the CIA funnels approximately half of its covert
military aid – worth approximately a billion dollars[45] – to the
figure of one Gulbuddin Hekmatyar. Lift the veil on this Islamic
fundamentalist terrorist and his brutal gang of murderous
guerrillas, and they turn out to be little more than an unofficial
branch of the Pakistani secret services (ISI), senior partner to
the CIA in the war against the Afghan revolution.[46] During the
1980s, Hekmatyar is a prolific and proven producer and
international distributer of heroin, personally owning at least six
large heroin refineries in the tribal regions bordering
Afghanistan, and controlling though corruption, terror and
intimidation a significant percentage of the region's opium
production.[47] If that doesn't make him repugnant enough as a

defender of freedom, according to *The New York Times*, as a young Islamic extremist, Hekmatyar 'despatched his followers to throw vials of acid into the faces of women students who refused to wear veils'.[48]

In case this revelation by that guardian of freedom, *The New York Times*, gives the wrong impression of the paper, it's worth noting that this article – and others finally exposing the real nature of the beast – doesn't appear until the end of a decade-long US-sponsored rampage of destruction, terrorism and drug-dealing, by which time the Soviet army have withdrawn from Afghanistan, leaving the country in the hands of some of the most backward despots and terrorists the world has ever seen; the most disciplined and well organised of these bands, by a mountain mile, being the Taliban. Before the Soviet withdrawal, the mainstream US press publishes only positive reports about Hekmatyar and his equally corrupt comrades in the loose alliance that is the mujahideen. By 1989, with the help of his supporters in the West, Hekmatyar has attained the lofty title of Foreign Minister of the Afghan Interim Government, by which time he is referred to as a criminal and a terrorist even by his own president.[49]

During the Afghan War, there are seventeen DEA agents posted at the US Embassy in Kabul. These diligent individuals duly compile detailed reports into the region's forty biggest heroin syndicates and distribute them among their superiors. Yet not one of these organisations is investigated over the whole decade-long period of war.[50] As early as 1982, Interpol is receiving reports that Pakistan's military leader, General Huq, is implicated in the heroin trade.[51] Pakistani and European police forces complain too that investigations into the heroin trade have 'been aborted at the highest level'.[52] By the end of the decade, the heroin trade is worth 8–10 billion dollars, more than the Pakistani government's annual budget, the equivalent of 25% of Pakistani GDP.[53]

As for crack, the story in Latin America is the twin of the Afghan tale, but without the bogeyman of Soviet communism to justify it.[54] Here, the US military and the CIA sponsor a savage and unpopular counter-revolutionary struggle against the widely respected Sandinista government in Nicaragua.[55]

In this bitter and bloody struggle, hundreds of schools and hospitals are destroyed, villages are burned, and civilians are raped and murdered by contra forces that US president Ronald Reagan ironically likens to the heroic French Resistance.[56] But despite Reagan's efforts to popularise these fascistic gangs, the respectable wing of US government is not fooled, and releases relatively little in the way of official military and financial aid. Predictably the financial pressures of this situation spawn the same demons as those already described in post-war France and Italy, Vietnam and China, but with cocaine – the raw material used to make crack – taking the place of heroin in the desperate cash-generation schemes.[57] While President Reagan gets busy blaming the Sandinistas and their allies for the international drug-dealing, his wife Nancy sponsors the famous 'Just Say No' campaign at home in the USA.

There is a shelf of books and papers on the origins of the western hemisphere's crack epidemic with titles such as: *Cocaine Politics: Drugs, Armies and the CIA in Central America*, and: *Dark Alliance: The CIA, the Contras and the Crack Cocaine Explosion*. Much of the material for this work has been explored and corroborated by US congressional hearings but still, somehow, the popular wisdom is that the US crack epidemic is caused mainly by poor black men in US ghettoes.[58]

Of course, there are a thousand ways to make the political history of smack and crack seem so complex and its meaning so nuanced as to be incomprehensible. After all, secrecy and plausible deniability are a crucial part of the political MO. But with an open mind, a dash of honesty and the right library, the truth is now fairly easy to discern. A significant part of this truth has to be that, although the CIA is undoubtedly the organisation with the single most direct overall responsibility for the worldwide growth in the use of hard drugs over the past several decades, not all the blame can be placed at the door of this venerable agency. It must be obvious even from this short history that the CIA in all its theatres is only doing what it has to do under the objective circumstances of fighting popular anti-capitalist movements of one kind or another when these fights are either illegal, unethical, or unpopular at home. Some proof of this is surely that the French and the American militaries both separately arrive at the same MO at the same time in the late 1940s and early 1950s, in Vietnam and Burma respectively. There are subtle differences between the two operations, for instance the French being more directly hands on and the CIA's more at one remove,[59] but the end result is the same: ruthless and determined counter-insurgency movements built on a foundation of drug-dealing.

Alas this bitter medicine can work wonders.

In the 1980s, the twin tsunamis of smack and crack produced by the CIA-sponsored and British-backed counter-revolutionary gangs in Asia and Latin America crash onto the dollar-rich shores of Europe and the USA. The profits dwarf those of the Golden Triangle era and grossly inflate the newly liberated global financial markets, especially its offshore branches. The accompanying deluge of hard drugs creates a living hell for millions in the ex-working class of the developed nations, drowning so many of the newly unemployed in the deadly milk of paradise, dazzling a lucky few with the shining but ephemeral trinkets of gangsterism.

And all the while our new world order inexorably takes shape.


*INTERESTING EXCEPTION: While the newly unemployed, poor and working-class youth of Western Europe and the USA are drowning in a sea of smack and crack from the early 1980s to the late 1990s, there is one place that completely bucks the trend for developed nations: the occupied six counties of the north of Ireland. During the period in question, responsibility for the policing of the poorest areas of the towns and cities of the region is directly in the hands of the poorest people themselves. On the streets of these areas, British government forces effectively have no writ.*

*During this period, Northern Ireland, as it is generally known, drug-using patterns for recreational drugs such as cannabis, amphetamines, LSD and ecstasy track pretty much exactly drug-using trends in the rest of the developed world. But according to the best evidence, the use of smack and crack is more or less zero.[60]*

## And Finally

To end on a personal note. The duty of a playwright is to provoke and entertain, but also to say things more respectable writers can't or won't say. So here's my own two-penneth:

Even our most stuffy, pro-capitalist historians would struggle to deny that, throughout the 1980s, at the international level, important and highly influential elements of the British state provide support and political cover for the drug-dealing, counter-revolutionary gangs in Afghanistan and Latin America.[61] But am I really suggesting these ruthless elements somehow conspire to start a hard-drug epidemic on the streets of Britain in the wake of the 1981 inner-city uprisings depicted in my play? I mean, they're not on the corner selling a bag, are they, these people from Eaton and Harrow and Cambridge and Sandhurst?

So, no. I'm not suggesting someone in the British government somewhere, even in the darkest corridor of power says aloud, 'Wouldn't it be marvellous if these damned inner-city youths, who are fighting us in their tens of thousands, burning our vehicles and creating a situation like the one we face in Northern Ireland, but on a far, far greater scale...[62] wouldn't it be marvellous if instead of fighting us and creating no-go areas, or even starting to govern themselves like they do in Catholic West Belfast, these youths sell and take drugs and, if they fight, they fight among themselves...' Of course not.

But in the context of the decades-long collusion summarised here between Western governments and drug-dealers and gangsters of all kinds – including myriad armed religious fanatics of varying faiths – almost always in the face of popular rebellion – and with this tendency reaching a historic peak in the early 1980s – there is an obvious question. And with rebellions and revolutions overrunning Africa, Asia and Latin America, when in 1981 fierce fighting suddenly breaks out in every major English city, personally I can't help but ask:

In that moment of grave crisis for the British ruling classes, when tens of thousands of people with nothing to lose – the likes of Neil and Mandy in my play, and the youths who 'took Liverpool that night' – stick a needle in their arm and melt away to nothing; when an entire generation turn from rebellion to petty crime, or gangsterism; when a couple of years later the defeated mining communities go the same way; and after that black and white inner-city youths start shooting and stabbing one another instead of fighting the power...

Do Margaret Thatcher and her cronies with their corporate backers and experienced military advisers give a flying fuck? Or are they secretly relieved?

Personally, I think they can't believe their luck.

*Ed Edwards*
*July 2018*

## Endnotes

1. Rees, L., *Auschwitz*, BBC Books, 2005.

2. McCoy, A.W., *The Politics of Heroin: CIA Complicity in the Global Drug Trade*. Lawrence Hill Books, 1991, pp. 24–39.

3. *Ibid.*, p. 28.

4. Block, A.A., *East Side, West Side: Organizing Crime in New York, 1930–1950*. Transaction Publishers, 1980.

5. Block; and many others.

6. Jacobs, J.B., *Mobsters, Unions, and Feds: The Mafia and the American Labor Movement*. NYU Press, 2007.

7. McCoy, pp. 31–8; and many others.

8. *Ibid.*, pp. 31–8.

9. Campbell, R., *The Luciano Project: The Secret Wartime Collaboration of the Mafia and the US Navy*. McGraw-Hill Companies, 1977; Newark, T., *Mafia Allies: The True Story of America's Secret Alliance with the Mob in World War II*. MBI Publishing Company, 2007; and many others.

10. Saunders, F.S., *Who Paid the Piper?: The CIA and the Cultural Cold War*, Granta Books, 2000.

11. Pieri, J., *The Octopus: The Rise and Rise of the Sicilian Mafia*. Birlinn, 2012.

12. *Ibid.*; and many others.

13. *Ibid.*

14. McCoy, pp. 31–8.

15. *Ibid.*

16. *Ibid.*, pp. 38–41.

17. Rees.

18. Hagen, Louis, *The Secret War for Europe,* Macdonald, 1968, pp. 21–48.

19. McCoy, p. 167. See also, for instance: *New York Times* 11/12/2010, 'Declassified Papers Show US Recruited Ex-Nazis'; and many others.

20. McCoy, pp. 51–3.

21. *Ibid.*, p. 60.

22. *Ibid.*, p. 62. In his memoire of the period, future CIA head William Colby says that in supporting Corsican gangsters of the day his organisation's personnel were, 'operating in the atmosphere of an order of Knights Templar, to save Western freedom from Communist darkness.' [William Colby, *Honourable Men: My Life in the CIA,* Simon and Schuster, 1978, p. 73.]

23. McCoy, p. 62.

24. *Ibid.*, pp. 60–63. Following his victory against the radical wing of the Marseilles Resistance, Defferre goes on to become a stalwart of post-war French politics for decades, oscillating between being a member of the National Assembly and Mayor of Marseilles until his death in 1986, including spells as Minster for Overseas France (1956–7) and Minister of Interior (1983–4). Defferre's protection of the Corsican underworld continues at least until 1967.

25. *Ibid.*, pp. 46–76.

26. *Ibid.*

27. Trinquier, R., *Modern Warfare*, Frederick Praeger, 1964; Kitson, F., *Low Intensity Operations: Subversion, Insurgency, Peace-keeping,* Faber & Faber, 1964.

28. Trinquier.

29. McCoy, p. 132 (equivalent calculations by Ed Edwards).

30. By 1915, as much as 25% of royal government taxes in Thailand (or Siam as it is then known) are raised from the distribution of opium to addicts smoking the drug in hundreds of Bangkok opium dens. [Virginia Thompson, *Thailand: The New Siam,* Macmillan, 1941, pp. 728–30.]

31. McCoy, p. 131.

32. *Ibid.*, p. 157.

33. Gravel, Mike, ed., *The Pentagon Papers: The Defence Department History of US Decision Making in Vietnam,* 5 vols. (Boston: Beacon Press, 1971).

34. McCoy, p. 251.

35. *Ibid.*, p. 161.

36. Kitson.

37. Snow, E., *Red Star Over China: The Classic Account of the Birth of Chinese Communism*, Atlantic Books, 2017.

38. Following the humiliation of the failed re-invasion of China, the CIA as we know it today was born through a merger of the various US wartime intelligence agencies, the biggest of which were the OSS and the new, more bureaucratic – and more stodgily conservative – CIA. The China fiasco and a number of embarrassing scandals caused by swashbuckling OSS officers, used to dealing with assorted ex-Gestapo officers and Corsican and Italian gangsters in Europe, made the merger a matter of national importance. The thing was, though, that in the newly consolidated organisation (all now under the umbrella name of the CIA), all the most important and influential positions were filled by the very reckless and swaggering old OSS hands like William Colby, who had been responsible for the previous humiliations. [John Ranelagh, *The Agency: The Rise and Decline of the CIA*, Simon and Schuster, 1986, pp. 134–35; William Colby, *Honourable Men: My Life in the CIA*, Simon and Schuster, 1978, p. 96.]

39. McCoy.

40. *Ibid*.

41. CNN Library, 27/3/18; and many others.

42. McCoy, pp. 222–6; and many others.

43. *Ibid*., pp. 259–61.

44. Scott, P.D. and Marshall, J., *Cocaine Politics: Drugs, Armies, and the CIA in Central America*. University of California Press, 1998, p. 69.

45. McCoy, p. 451.

46. *Ibid*., p. 449.

47. *Ibid*., p. 454.

48. *New York Times Magazine*, 4/2/1990.

49. McCoy, p. 453.

50. *Ibid*., p. 454.

51. *Ibid*.

52. *Ibid*.

53. *Ibid*., p. 457.

54. It's often assumed that the Soviet invasion was the cause of the US and therefore the CIA's involvement in the covert war against the Afghan regime that gave rise to worldwide heroin explosion of the 1980s. However, the truth is the US/CIA support for the terroristic narcotic-dealing Islamic fundamentalist gangs (that later became known as the mujahideen) came first. In the words of Jimmy Carter's National Security Advisor, Zbigniew Brzezinski:

According to the official version of history, CIA aid to the Mujahadeen began during 1980, that is to say, after the Soviet army invaded Afghanistan, 24 Dec 1979. But the reality, secretly guarded until now, is completely otherwise: Indeed, it was July 3, 1979 that President Carter signed the first directive for secret aid to the opponents of the pro-Soviet regime in Kabul. And that very day, I wrote a note to the president in which I explained to him that in my opinion this aid was going to induce a Soviet military intervention. ['Le Nouvel Observateur' (France), Jan 15--1, 1998, p. 76.]

55. Scott and Marshall; and Webb, G., *Dark Alliance: The CIA, the Contras, and the Cocaine Explosion*, Seven Stories Press, 2011.

56. *Washington Post*, 31/3/86.

57. The difficulties faced by the US military in raising funds for the Sandinistas are one of the major factors leading to what became known as 'The War on Drugs'. The policy was conceived at least in part because, each time the US military faced a threat from popular revolutionary forces in Latin America (or indeed elsewhere in the world), they had to build a separate case in front of Congress to raise money for their often brutal and unpopular proxy counterforces. In each case, the US military met with similar resistance from liberals, or left, or church and human-rights activists. The situation in Colombia provided US military strategists with a golden opportunity to overturn this whole process. In Colombia, popular support for the opposition guerrilla movement, the largest faction of which was the FARC, was found mainly among the poorest peasants. A large number of the poorest peasants of Colombia were and still are forced by economic necessity to grow the coca leaves necessary to feed the crack explosion in North America. These poor peasants benefitted not one jot from the super-profits being generated at the international level by the gangsters and right-wing militia who were buying the leaves from them for refining and distribution. The peasants themselves remained wretchedly poor, and very often supported the resistance movements fighting the central power. The central power itself, of course, is supported by the USA and often by the very right-wing militia who are refining and exporting the cocaine. US military strategists realised that, if they could label the guerrilla wings of the people's resistance movements of the region 'Narcoterrorists', because in part they represented the poor coca-leaf growers, it would be more difficult for Congress/liberal/left/church people to support them. US Special Forces commander, Col. John D. Waghelstein, argued in a well-respected security journal that if this connection could be made,

> …in the public's mind and in Congress […] Congress would find it difficult to stand in the way of supporting our allies [like the contras] […] Those church and academic groups that have slavishly supported insurgency in Latin America would find themselves on the wrong side of the moral issue. Above all, we would have the unassailable moral position from which to launch a concerted effort using Department of Defence (DOD) assets [US military forces] and non-DOD assets [mercenary militias] Instead of wading through the legislative snarl and financial constraints […] we could act with alacrity.
> [Waghelstein quoted in Dale and Scott *Cocaine Politics*]

Put more honestly: we can use international drug-dealing as an excuse to support international drug-dealers.

58. For an in-depth analysis of the political association in USA of black people with drug use – despite their being statistically less likely than whites to either use or deal drugs – see Alexander, Michelle. *The New Jim Crow: Mass Incarceration in the Age of Colorblindness* [The New Press, 2012]. Alexander traces the origins of the modern politicisation of hard drugs in USA to Nixon's declaration of a war on drugs in 1974. Nixon's advisors later admitted that the idea was a ploy to win the racist vote in the south, where it was well understood that 'War on Drugs' meant war on black people. Such a ploy was required by 1974 because, in the wake of the Civil Rights Movement, open racism was no longer publicly acceptable. Michelle Alexander is the main contributor to the must-see Netflix documentary, *13th*.

59. McCoy, p. 130, and many others.

60. Parker, H., 'Use of Illegal Drugs in Northern Ireland', in Strang, A. & Gossop, M. (eds), *Heroin*, Routledge, 2005.

61. Even as late as 1991, with the Taliban carrying out opium-eradication programmes in Afghanistan, Tony Blair et al order the 2001 invasion of Afghanistan using the Northern Alliance, a proxy army of known drug-dealers, gangsters and terrorists. Interestingly, Blair cites two main war aims: to crush the heroin trade, and to improve the lot of women. Over the next six years to 2007, Afghanistan's opium production grows by 4,500% to become approximately 53% of the nation's GDP (NB At the height of the Colombian cartels' supremacy, cocaine production only ever reaches about 3% of Colombia's GDP). On the other front, the British-backed president of the country, Hamid Karzai (an ex-oil exec) introduces a law legalising rape within marriage and preventing women from leaving the house without permission.

[For more on Northern Alliance drug-dealing see: *Guardian* 9/1/18 'How the heroin trade explains the UK-US Failure in Afghanistan', and *Huffington Post* 15/11/08, 'How Deeply is the US involved in the Afghan Drug Trade?' For the GDP and opium production figures see: *Tom Dispatch* 30/03/2010 'Afghanistan as a Drug War', by Alfred W. McCoy. For the law about rape see: *Daily Telegraph* 26/6/18, 'Hamid Karzai signs law 'legalising rape in marriage'].

62. It's worth saying in this context that the thirty-year-long war in Ireland was mostly fought by fractions of the populations of Belfast and Derry, only the seventeenth and eightieth largest population centres of the UK. The 1981 uprisings took place in six or seven of the top ten.

**Further Reading**

Alfred W. McCoy, *The Politics of Heroin*. Big fat must-read on the subject for exhaustive detail, every last twist and turn over nearly a century. Most of the above is shaped by McCoy's towering work.

Peter Dale Scott and Jonathan Marshall, *Cocaine Politics: Drugs, Armies, and the CIA in Central America*. Univ of California Press; again exhaustive, largely drawn from the work of US congressional hearings into the Latin American situation.

Gary Webb (R.I.P), *Dark Alliance: The CIA, The Contras and the Crack Cocaine Explosion*. Forensic and massive on detail.

Nick Schou, *Shoot the Messenger*. The story of how Journalist Gary Webb (see above) was hounded to his death – partly by the big hitters in the US print media – for trying to tell the truth about the link between CIA assets in Latin America and the crack explosion. The book is better than the recent film of the same name telling the same story.

The last book is probably the easiest to read, the first is the best.

**A Nick Hern Book**

*The Political History of Smack and Crack* first published in Great Britain as a paperback original in 2018 by Nick Hern Books Limited, The Glasshouse, 49a Goldhawk Road, London W12 8QP, in association Most Wanted, Offstage Theatre and W14 Productions

Cover image © MattTullett/Photographydept.com 2016

Designed and typeset by Nick Hern Books, London
Printed in Great Britain by Mimeo Ltd, Huntingdon, Cambridgeshire PE29 6XX

A CIP catalogue record for this book is available from the British Library

ISBN 978 1 84842 781 5

**www.nickhernbooks.co.uk**

facebook.com/nickhernbooks

twitter.com/nickhernbooks